ITALIAN INTERIORS

ITALIAN INTERIORS

ROOMS WITH A VIEW

LAURA MAY TODD

Contents

Introduction

In 1928, the renowned Milanese architect and designer Gio Ponti published an essay on what he believed constituted the Italian house. 'La Casa all'Italiana' formed the foreword of the first ever issue of *Domus*, the architecture and design magazine he founded that year, which would go on to dictate and document the currents of the international and Italian design industry throughout the twentieth and twenty-first centuries – it is still going strong today.

In his essay, Ponti described the quintessential Italian house, first by distinguishing it from homes found in neighbouring countries:

> 'The Italian house is not a refuge, padded and garnished by its inhabitants against the harshness of the climate, as are the dwellings beyond the Alps where residents seek shelter from inclement nature for long months: the Italian house is the place chosen by us to enjoy our life, with joyful possession, the beauties that our lands and our skies give us in the long seasons.'

He went on to investigate the relationship between a home's interior and exterior. 'Not a great distinction', according to Ponti, who argued that features such as pergolas, verandas and loggias are all so intrinsically Italian as to be known by those (Italian) names in almost every language.

His main claim, however, was that a home should serve the needs of its inhabitants in more than just a functional sense. 'Its design does not descend solely from the material needs of living', he wrote – it is not just 'a machine to inhabit'. The house should be a repository for life: a place where objects delight and provide comfort.

In researching, editing and writing this book, I've thought a lot about what makes an Italian house Italian, and I have a few theories. An Italian house, as you will see in the following pages, is one that lives in harmony with history, whose objects and furnishings speak to the ideas and passions of its occupants; it is a space that, despite the preciousness of the objects that reside within, is intentionally configured to welcome others inside.

It has been almost a century since Ponti first penned his essay, and the idea of what makes a house 'Italian' – if one could ever truly make that distinction – has no doubt evolved. Indeed, Ponti was only thirty-seven when he wrote 'La Casa all'Italiana', but he would continue to design homes, furniture and skyscrapers into his eighties. It can be assumed – and, in fact, it is clear – that his tastes evolved from these early dictums, especially considering the radical cultural and political shift that followed World War II. While Ponti couldn't predict the future, what he did do was lay down the opening arguments for a conversation that is still being held today. Within the pages of this book, you will find homes both occupied and conceived by some of the most celebrated figures of contemporary Italian design.

With each example of their work, we can discern their ideas of how to live and what they, too, have contributed to this decades-long dialogue.

Take Studio Peregalli, who used antique materials to transform a humble cottage into a stunning retreat on the island of Capri (*see page 108*). What the studio's founders, Roberto Peregalli and Laura Sartori Rimini, seem to tell us is that, with the right sensibility, the allure of the past can be carved out from the mundane. Architect Massimiliano Locatelli's industrial-looking outpost in Puglia (*see page 200*) suggests, through its utilitarian metal furniture and spartan decoration, that precision and economy do not preclude luxury. Then there is the decadent Venetian palazzo occupied by the architect Vincenzo De Cotiis (*see page 28*), where the demands of life become secondary to the grander purpose of coexisting with art.

Each of these designers works on the international stage, pushing what we consider the canon of Italian design and decoration into new territory. But this book also explores earlier homes that remain touchstones of Italian design. For example, architect Piero Portaluppi's Villa Necchi Campiglio in Milan (*see page 40*), the designer Carlo Mollino's secret lair in Turin (*see page 90*) and the painter Giacomo Balla's apartment in Rome (*see page 156*). These spaces have been preserved exactly as those who created them intended and can be visited as house museums, allowing a rare glimpse into private domains that are usually sequestered behind closed doors.

So what does this eclectic array of homes – all equally impressive but wildly different – tell us about the singular notion of the Italian house? How do we discern the thread that connects them? In my view, an Italian house exhibits an unwavering fidelity to personal vision. It is the expression of a point of view, a vision for the future and a thesis for how to live.

Later in his career, Ponti would break from the bourgeois propriety described in 'La Casa all'Italiana' and introduce more radical concepts into his work. My personal favourite among his projects of this period is Casa Lucano, also known as Casa di Fantasia (*see page 18*).

In 1953, Ponti was commissioned to design an apartment in Milan for Mario and Lisetta Lucano, the owners of a successful electronics company. The couple were avid collectors and patrons of the arts, so they allowed Ponti carte blanche to come up with the wildest, most artistic concept he could. Captivated by the French Surrealist and Italian Metaphysical artists of the era, Ponti explored how architecture could manipulate perception in the same way as, say, a painting by Giorgio de Chirico. In the sitting room, he hung drapes printed with floating hot-air balloons by the designer Piero Fornasetti. The artist Edina Altara painted mythical, fresco-like figures on mirror-fronted furniture and interior glass doors. The home's crown jewel was the elaborate *boiserie*, depicting a lithographically printed trompe-l'oeil library complete with drawings of Grecian urns, playing cards and esoteric statuettes, also by Fornasetti, which was broken up by panels of swirling walnut-burl veneer.

In 2019, after the contents of the home had been dismantled and sold at auction, the Lebanese design studio David/Nicolas, founded by David Raffoul and Nicolas Moussallem, was tasked with reinventing the empty apartment in a way that paid tribute to Ponti's masterpiece. Their design beautifully bridged the eras. In responding to the *boiserie*, they came up with an abstract interpretation of the original burl veneer, using inlaid wood in shapes that resemble soft, gestural brushstrokes. In lieu of Fornasetti's illustrations of bursting bookshelves, they designed a real shelving system lined with burgundy silk – creating a dialogue with the past.

In a way, a similar conversation is being conducted in nearly every project in this book. Italy is a country that forces you to live with its history and most of these homes reside in structures that were built decades or, more often, centuries ago. Many lived several lives before assuming their current state: you'll find former convents, embassies, farmhouses and even a textile mill.

When I moved to Italy in 2016, I had only visited the country a handful of times. I grew up in a context that couldn't be more different, in a cookie-cutter suburban home on the outskirts of a Canadian city where ground was broken on the first buildings just over one hundred years ago. Confronting the vastness of Italy's cultural history was daunting, but writing about its homes felt like a clear path to understanding the country and the people within it. Luckily, I had landed in Milan, where the brightest design minds have convened ever since Ponti founded *Domus*.

I got to know the country by stepping through its heavy wooden doorways, peering into private bedrooms and kitchens, and sipping espresso from tiny porcelain *tazze* in cavernous, fresco-adorned living rooms and on quiet terraces. I learned that for those who care deeply about living in a thoughtful way, every object has a story. The things with which one lives – whether they be century-old antiques or functional utensils – aren't meant to be left on a shelf and looked at for a lifetime but rather used, cared for, and, most importantly, shared.

In making this book, it was important for me to include spaces by those who are not conventionally thought of as designers. You'll find artist Maro Gorky's resplendent Tuscan farmhouse (*see page 118*), the walls of which are adorned with her vibrant landscape paintings. There's the Sicilian *masseria* owned by Riccardo Priolis and John Hooks (*see page 112*), which became the canvas for their explorations into Classical art and Sicilian craft. Even more than a monumental design or a captivating history, it's my belief that the Italian home is rendered beautiful simply by the manner in which one is welcomed into it.

The more time I spend in this country, the more sure I am of that fact. When I first walked up to the modern grey building that houses Kenny Spooren and Andrea Zanatelli's flat (*see page 102*), I had trouble reconciling the stark concrete facade with the treasure trove I knew lay within – I had seen photos of the wealth of curious antiques the couple were amassing in their two-bedroom apartment on the west side of Milan. When I finally walked through the door and saw these objects up close, I understood their passion and attention to detail. On a later visit, the couple spent hours telling me about their trips to historic houses across Europe, where they seek inspiration, and the markets in Italy and Belgium where they source their finds. Meanwhile, simmering on the stovetop was a homemade *ragù*, which we ate by candlelight, flickering shadows cast across the sculptures, textiles and curiosities that make up the couple's collection.

It was a similar story the first morning I visited the former lumber workshop that houses the home and studio of architect Roberto Gerosa (*see page 146*). Sitting at the kitchen island (made of an old discarded door he found when he moved in), we enjoyed green tea and ginger biscuits as he told me about the first sculptural lamps he designed in the 1980s and the time fashion designer Diane von Furstenberg wandered into a West Village gallery and bought a glowing paper moon of his for her Manhattan penthouse. He showed me how he fashions the lamps by hand in the basement studio and how he draws out the plans for the homes he designs, sketching the leafy palms, patterned carpets and crystal chandeliers by hand. As we talked, a plume of smoke from a stick of burning incense left a haze hanging in the air, adding to the atmosphere of exoticism in the post-industrial space.

It was nearly a century ago that Ponti made his declarations on the Italian house, yet I believe his thesis stands the test of time. He put it best: 'The Italian house', he wisely wrote, 'is the place chosen by us to enjoy our life.'

Laura May Todd

1 The spiral oak staircase of La Filanda, a house on Lake Como designed by Luca Guadagnino (*see page 12*). 2 Masseria Cardinale's stone courtyard in Noto, Sicily (*see page 112*). 3 Design studio David/Nicolas's reinterpretation of Gio Ponti's Casa di Fantasia in Milan. (*see page 18*). 4 Maro Gorky's Tuscan farmhouse (*see page 118*).

A theatrical and colour-saturated lake house

Lake Como, Lombardy
Luca Guadagnino

Film director Luca Guadagnino's films are known for a certain atmosphere of rarified Italian-ness. His 2017 film *Call Me By Your Name* centres on a picturesque villa in the Lombard hinterlands, while his 2009 masterpiece *I Am Love* leans sumptuously into its location, Milan's Villa Necchi Campiglio (*see page 40*). When Guadagnino opened his own interior design firm in 2018, enthusiasts were eager to see the captivating spaces he would dream up for clients. His first project, La Filanda – the restyling of a century-old silk-weaving factory perched on the western shore of Lake Como – did not disappoint. Guadagnino brought all of his powers of narrative, scenography and aesthetic sensibility to this family home.

Owners, fashion entrepreneur Federico Marchetti and journalist Kerry Olsen wanted a place where they could enjoy the serenity of the lake with their daughter. Working with a team of 150 craftsmen, Guadagnino transformed the two-story, modernist-style building into a masterwork of Italian artisanry. On the walls

of the entranceway, fluted oak panelling with reflective brass inserts sets the tone. A gilt-bronze mirror by famed French sculptor and designer Claude Lalanne hangs to the right of the door, breaking up the *boiserie's* vertical lines. This oak wall detailing carries through the entire house: it winds around the curving central staircase, then through the hallways towards the bedrooms, office, library and underground pool.

In the living room, the fluted wainscoting ends halfway up the wall, giving way to a repeating pattern of turmeric- and mustard-toned textile panels. The colour becomes more vibrant as the eye rises, the barrel-vaulted roof finished with an acidic shade of green. Guadagnino, Marchetti and Olsen are all keen connoisseurs of fine craft and storied design and here their passions came together in the form of scores of exquisite objects including a table by George Nakashima, mahogany chairs by Kaare Klint, and a custom marble table from Hermès.

1 A pair of playful chandeliers by designer Michael Anastassiades welcome guests at the entrance of La Filanda. 2 The basement pool takes inspiration from nautical tropes. 3 In the dining room a tiered Piero Fornasetti chandelier hangs above a custom marble table by Hermès. 4 The laundry room features floor to ceiling matte lacquered cabinets in a variety of green shades. 5 An abstract painting in the master bedroom compliments vibrant rugs by French brand Cogolin.

A theatrical and colour-saturated lake house

A design icon's masterpiece reinterpreted

Milan
Gio Ponti
& David/Nicolas

Casa di Fantasia is widely considered one of renowned Milanese architect and designer Gio Ponti's most daring and creative works. Set in what was, at the time, one of Milan's tallest buildings, the apartment was designed for art-collecting couple Mario and Lisetta Lucano in 1953 (and is also known as Casa Lucano). Ponti took inspiration for the interiors from Surrealist paintings and Metaphysical art.

Conceived to feel like stepping inside a living stage set, its walls were lined with lithograph-printed panels by famed illustrator Piero Fornasetti, depicting heaving trompe l'oeil bookshelves, and the custom furniture was decorated with mythological illustrations by designer Edina Altara. The apartment remained almost entirely intact for nearly seventy years, until 2019, when it was sold and its fantastical contents sent to auction. An art collector named Michele Marocchino bought the empty shell and endeavoured to remake it in a way that paid homage to its incredible past life.

Marocchino commissioned Milan-based studio David/Nicolas, led by David Raffoul and Nicolas Moussallem – who both grew up in Beirut but moved their practice to Milan in 2019 – to design a contemporary interpretation of Ponti's masterpiece. In designing the space, the duo reimagined the original fabulist concoction with their own sense of retro-futuristic style.

Where Fornasetti's lithograph-printed *boiserie* once stood, the duo installed French oak panels inlaid with dynamic markings resembling tiger print, or custom modular shelving upholstered with burgundy silk. Though Ponti's masterpiece had largely been stripped bare (down to the door handles, which Marocchino was able to recover at auction), they kept original details where possible – the bubblegum-pink bathtub; the cloudy white-and-grey marble floors; the honey-coloured ash walls – resulting in a unique union of Italy's old masters and contemporary talent.

A design icon's masterpiece reinterpreted

A design icon's masterpiece reinterpreted

1 The French oak *boiserie* is decorated with inlay resembling tiger stripes. 2 A series of drawings by Italian artist Carole Rama hangs above the bed. 3 Ponti played with perspective throughout the apartment, employing tricks often used in stage design. 4 The front door was designed to look as though it is floating off its hinges. 5 When owner Michele Marocchino purchased the house, he discovered the original bathroom tiles hidden under a carpet: they were removed and affixed to the wall as part of the redesign.

A rationalist apartment with sweeping sea views

Naples
Giuliano Andrea dell'Uva

Naples often feels like a planet apart from the rest of Italy. The baroque southern city has its own distinct culture, music and even language – visiting feels like entering an entirely different, more frenetic world. Wander through narrow cobblestone streets of the Spanish quarter, and you'll hear streams of Neapolitan dialect mingling with the conventional Italian, as mopeds roar past your elbows and housewives chatter to each other out of windows overhead. Travel just a few miles west along the Gulf of Naples, however, and you'll reach Posillipo, a quiet residential area populated by stately villas and lush Mediterranean gardens. It is here that architect Giuliano Andrea dell'Uva has reimagined an apartment located in a 1950s rationalist-style building originally designed by the Polish architect David Pacanowski, a mentee of renowned Swiss modernist Le Corbusier.

The architect's objective for the apartment was to create a stylistic continuity with the building's original design without losing sight of contemporary

influences. Throughout the house, he has deftly balanced proportion, colour and lines: sinuous dove-grey Osaka sofas by Pierre Paulin play against the strict rationalist geometry; in the primary bedroom a puzzle-like coloured tile floor mural by the artist David Tremlett adds depth and movement to the all-white room; a built-in aluminium bed frame in the guest bedroom adds a 'techno' edge to the home's impressive original materials, like the blue-veined marble in the entranceway and bathroom.

In the living room, dell'Uva preserved a ceramic panel by a local artist, the handmade texture of which provides an organic contrast to the room's clean lines and minimal atmosphere. The panel depicts an abstracted panorama of the island of Capri – an artistic interpretation of the spectacular scene outside the apartment's wide picture windows, which boast sweeping views over the bay and the islands beyond.

1 A ceramic relief depicting Capri and the Bay of Naples was left *in-situ* on the wall.
2 A pair of Osaka sofas by Pierre Paulin snake across the living room. 3 The bathroom
is entirely clad in blue-grey marble as a nod to the original stone floor in the apartment's
entranceway. 4 dell'Uva installed a striking aluminium hearth in the main living space.

A rationalist apartment with sweeping sea views

A baroque palazzo where past and present overlap

Venice
Vincenzo De Cotiis

Palazzo Giustinian Lolin sits along the curving banks of Venice's Grand Canal, just before the waterway passes beneath the wooden arc of the Ponte dell'Accademia and empties into the lagoon. Like many of the city's magnificent old *palazzi*, its foundations can be traced back to the fifteenth century, but its current iteration, including its Classical facade in white marble, is attributed to the seventeenth-century architect Baldassare Longhena. A host of aristocrats and luminaries have called its various apartments home over the years, but since 2019, the *piano nobile*, or main floor, has been the occasional residence of architect Vincenzo De Cotiis and his wife, Claudia Rosa.

The work of De Cotiis, which spans furniture, interior design and art, is often described as monumental, a term that fits naturally into the spectacular context of a Venetian palazzo. His furnishings, made of rare and colourful marbles, precious metals or even industrial cast-offs, are

hewn so as to retain the patina of the original materials. They are set against centuries-old *terrazzo* flooring and wooden beams that have weathered and warped in the salty air, establishing an era-defying sense of kinship. Indeed, it is a rare feat for a contemporary designer to take on the immensity of Venetian decadence yet still find harmony within the excess. As of April 2024, Palazzo Giustinian Lolin became the Vincenzo de Cotiis Foundation, a contemporary art and design exhibition space.

A baroque palazzo where past and present overlap

A baroque palazzo where past and present overlap

1 The monolithic bed is made from recycled fibreglass, which has been painted with a textured pattern. 2 A slab of green malachite challant stone forms the top of the sculptural dining table designed by de Cotiis. 3 An antique Venetian chandelier in the living room. 4 The custom sink in the bathroom is hewn from breccia baixa marble. 5 Original silk brocade fabric lines the walls of the study. 6 In the bathroom, a Carlo Bugatti chair from 1895 sits next to the window, made of classic Venetian roundel glass.

A coastal cottage built into the landscape

Costa Paradiso, Sardinia
Alberto Ponis
& Ivan Baj

The architect Alberto Ponis was born in Genoa in 1933, but the majority of his work is found across the sea in Sardinia, Italy's largest island. Physically wild and culturally distant from the mainland, Sardinia captivates with its rugged beauty and unique traditions. In 1994, the glass artist Ivan Baj commissioned Ponis to design a home for him on a stretch of *macchia mediterranea* – the rocky scrubland typical of Italy's coastal regions – in Costa Paradiso, a picturesque hamlet on the island's northern shore. The house, named Casa Stella for its distinctive, star-shaped footprint, sits wedged among a cluster of pink boulders overlooking the sea. The home feels as if it is carved directly into the earth.

Massive rocks are left balanced *in situ* in the interior, emerging from the whitewashed plaster walls and the mosaic of granite tiles on the floor. There is no furniture in the house. Instead, furnishings are built directly into the structure: wide steps become sofas; carved alcoves lined with white handmade cushions

are used as beds. Inspired by the humble cottages on the Greek island of Patmos, the house is decorated sparsely with simple but elegant objects. Ceramics by Pablo Picasso are arranged in niches along the walls, as well as Baj's poetic, handblown glasswork. But the home's true beauty is its open communication with the surrounding landscape. The Mediterranean sun enters through the wide terrace doors, illuminating Ponis's masterful and organic design.

A coastal cottage built into the landscape

Costa Paradiso, Sardinia

1 The view from the living room towards the terrace with sweeping views across the azure sea. 2 Built-in sofas and a day bed in the living room. 3 Local pink granite flagstones line the floor of the home. 4 The dining table and wraparound seating are also built into the architecture. 5 Baj's collection of glass and ceramics in the kitchen.

A coastal cottage built into the landscape

A cinematic urban villa that continues to inspire

Milan
Piero Portaluppi

Villa Necchi Campiglio was conceived in 1935 by Milan's pre-eminent architect at the time, Piero Portaluppi, and upon its completion, was widely considered the city's finest modern house. Commissioned by the Necchi family – wealthy industrialists who had made their fortune producing sewing machines – the home was built in the rationalist style, which marries the clean, minimal lines of modernism with forms that pay homage to Classical architecture, and no expense was spared in its furnishings.

In the ground-floor dining room, parchment-covered walls hung with sixteenth-century Belgian tapestries reach upwards to a ceiling inscribed with astrological imagery. The entranceway's walnut and rosewood *boiserie* follows the marble staircase up to the second floor. Imposing decorative steel doors separate the glassed-in veranda from the rest of the house. Surrounded by a walled garden bursting with pastel hydrangeas and endless wisteria vines, the tranquil estate feels like a quiet island within the bustling metropolis.

Almost a century later, Villa Necchi remains a touchstone of Milanese design and continues to be a reference point for contemporary designers. The house has even been immortalized in popular culture: several films, including Luca Guadagnino's *I Am Love*, have been filmed here. The house has been preserved in its original state and is now a museum, allowing visitors to witness its extravagant beauty first-hand.

A cinematic urban villa that continues to inspire

A cinematic urban villa that continues to inspire

1 Textured glass windows diffuse the light in Portaluppi's design. 2 A sculpture by Arturo Martini sits at the bottom of the grand central staircase. 3 The home sits in the centre of a sprawling private garden, which also boasts the first private swimming pool built in Milan. 4 The glassed-in veranda features a custom curved sofa and double-glazed windows with space for potted plants between the panes. 5 Parchment lines the walls of the dining room. 6 A giant porthole window in the bathroom.

A 16th-century home reworked by a pair of renowned architects

Monselice, Veneto
Carlo Scarpa
& Tobia Scarpa

The sixteenth-century architect Andrea Palladio was the progenitor of what is now known as the Palladian style. Born in Padua in 1508, Palladio would go on to build scores of extravagant villas in the Veneto countryside. Defined by an adherence to symmetry and generous use of Classical detailing, the style remained popular until the eighteenth century in Italy and abroad. Il Palazzetto – a villa in Monselice, a village close to Padua – was built in the mid-1600s following Palladian principles. The facade of the 800 m2 (8,611 sq ft), three-story, cuboid building is graced with Doric columns topped with arched pediments, while inside, rooms with soaring, six-metre- (twenty-foot-) high ceilings are decorated with allegorical frescos.

When Aldo Businaro inherited the villa from his grandfather in 1964, he was determined to restore it as a family home – it had been in use primarily as a storehouse for the surrounding farm – and commissioned renowned Venetian architect Tobia Scarpa to modernize parts of the structure. Scarpa's

intervention created a kitchen from a former store-room and reimagined the grand central hearth. A few years later, after a chance meeting with Tobia's father, Carlo – among the greatest of the twentieth-century Italian masters – Businaro asked the elder Scarpa to revisit the project. Carlo's contributions to the house consisted of designing an outdoor dining room and converting the barn into a liveable space. The most elaborate alteration, however, was completed long after the architect's death in 1978: a cast concrete external staircase that flows from the driveway to the first-floor window was commissioned by Businaro's children and was completed by Tobia in 2006.

Aldo, a longtime sales consultant for historic Italian design brands, furnished the home to reflect his own interests and passions: important pieces by both Scarpas, furniture from twentieth-century designers like Erik Gunnar Asplund and Le Corbusier, and a vast collection of modern art now sit comfortably alongside the dramatic Renaissance decorations.

A 16th-century home reworked by a pair of renowned architects

Monselice, Veneto

1 Carlo Scarpa designed the colourful geometric sliding door on the former barn.
2 The family's collection of artwork on the living room wall. 3 A selection of furniture
by 20th-century icons in the office space. 4 The dining room features Carlo Scarpa's
splitback chairs from the 1970s. 5 Exquisite 16th-century frescoes adorn the Palladian
villa's walls.

A 16th-century home reworked by a pair of renowned architects

Monselice, Veneto

A 1940s apartment that pays homage to its past

Milan
Carlo Perillo d'Albore
& Fabio Ceresa

Rationalism was a popular building style in Italy in the early twentieth century and it forms a significant chapter in the history of Italian architecture. Influenced by the modernist movement, rationalist buildings are scant on superficial embellishment and decoration and are instead characterized by the use of expensive materials such as marble, hardwood and brass. The style found favour in public buildings and urban planning projects from the 1920s to the 1940s, but because of the political beliefs of many of its proponents, it became closely associated with Benito Mussolini's Fascist regime, which embraced the style as a symbol of power and authority.

Constructed in 1941, this apartment owned by lawyer Carlo Perillo d'Albore and playwright and opera director Fabio Ceresa, sits perched at the top of a seven-story rationalist-style building in Milan. When they first acquired the space, they found the original frosted interior doors and oak parquet flooring still intact. They were entranced by its spectacular

views: light pours in from large windows, while balconies and terraces offer panoramas of both the city and the Alps.

In designing the house, they found inspiration in the architectural masterpieces of the era, including two of Piero Portaluppi's most revered residential projects: Villa Necchi Campiglio (*see page 40*) and Casa Boschi Di Stefano. The dark-green marble bathroom with its black lacquer vanity and circular mirror recalls Villa Necchi's luxurious en suites, while the cross-hatched moulded ceiling references Casa Boschi Di Stefano's entranceway. The motif is also echoed in the inlaid marble floors. The art and furniture are a mix of pieces from the couple's previous homes and new items bought together. Furniture acquired from the palace of Casapulla in the province of Caserta is set against a modern, cherry-coloured four-poster bed. Baroque craftsmanship alternates with twentieth-century design, and art objects range from antiquity to the present age, reflecting the eclectic tastes of the owners.

A 1940s apartment that pays homage to its past

1 A Franco Albini rattan armchair in the library. 2 The living room boasts a pair of Guglielmo Ulrich art deco chairs from the 1930s and a 1980s Willy Rizzo coffee table. 3 A varnished steel canopy bed by Xam creates a striking contrast with the petrol-blue walls of the bedroom. 4 In the kitchen, an Eero Saarinen dining table and Gae Aulenti Locus Solus chrome chairs. 5 The bathroom of Piero Portaluppi's Villa Necchi Campiglio (*see page 45*)was the inspiration behind this marble-lined room.

A 1940s apartment that pays homage to its past

An aristocratic palazzo transformed for modern living

Florence
b-arch

Throughout the Renaissance, the powerful and wealthy Florentine dynasties competed with each other, each trying to build the most elaborate and sumptuous residence. Scores of these extravagantly rendered palaces have been faithfully preserved as museums and can be visited by the public, but the city is still teeming with incredible examples of Renaissance architecture that remain private homes kept behind closed doors.

In 2017, Prato-based architecture studio b-arch was commissioned to transform Palazzo Spinelli, located on Florence's left bank, into a pied-à-terre for the owners of an Italian fashion brand. According to historical records, the palazzo was completed in 1470 by the Renaissance architect Bernardo Rossellino for the noble Spinelli family, who made their fortune in banking. The palazzo's original architecture is characterized by ornate botanical carvings on the facade, an internal courtyard bordered by shady loggia, and detailed frescoes on the interior walls

that have faded beautifully with time. It was the architects' task to preserve these ancient features while setting them up in dialogue with contemporary counterparts.

In the kitchen, for instance, gold panels decorated with leafy illustrations were installed to echo the patterns on the building's facade. Meanwhile, the chosen furniture – a modular de Sede Snake sofa from the 1970s, a Sputnik chandelier and a vintage brass coffee table – blends seamlessly with the muted patina of the frescoed walls and terracotta floors, deftly saturating this centuries-old palazzo with a sophisticated brand of contemporary style.

1 A modular de Sede sofa and a Sputnik-style chandelier give this ancient palazzo a contemporary twist. 2 The restored faux marble walls and *cotto* ceramic flooring date from the 15th century. 3 Intricate *graffito* etchings decorate the building's facade. 4 Artist Elena Carozzi hand-painted the gold-toned panels in the kitchen.

An aristocratic palazzo transformed for modern living

An architect's playful former farmhouse

Lecce, Puglia
Mirta Ottaviani

In the sun-bleached region of Puglia, everything is white. Walls, streets and facades of houses all glisten under the Mediterranean sun, and not without reason: traditionally, these surfaces were finished with a glossy white limewash in order to reflect the sun's harsh rays, keeping cities and towns cool even as temperatures soar.

This blank canvas provided the perfect backdrop for the creative vision of Roman designer Mirta Ottaviani. She undertook the transformation of a farmhouse near the town of Lecce, turning it into a family retreat characterized by contrasting pops of vibrant colour and striking graphic patterns. According to Ottaviani, she was inspired by the region's melting-pot history: Puglia's strategic location along important trade routes has meant that, historically, cultures from across the Mediterranean have left their mark on this land.

Organized in an 'L' shape around a shady garden, the rooms all open onto the outdoors.

Indeed, the garden functions as its own room in the house. Puglia is usually warm, with very little rainfall, meaning outdoor living is possible all year long. Ottaviani took advantage of this by installing an outdoor kitchen, where turquoise textile cabinet fronts and a chequerboard worktop create a harmonious interplay with the geometric decorations at the home's perimeter. The farmhouse, where the boundaries between indoor and outdoor spaces blur, captures a unique blend of history and modern living.

1 Colourful textiles, including the built-in sofa's striped upholstery, pop against the bone-white walls. 2 The wide courtyard and shaded porch facilitate indoor-outdoor living. 3 Vaulted ceilings are a typical feature of Puglian homes. 4 All of the rooms in the building have direct access to the outdoor space.

An architect's playful former farmhouse

Lecce, Puglia

A soulful restoration where the walls became a canvas

Arezzo, Tuscany
Roberto Baciocchi

The Tuscan architect Roberto Baciocchi – best known for his long-time collaboration with Prada, having designed many stores for the brand across the globe – has a way of injecting soul into even the most sterile of spaces. Baciocchi hails from Arezzo, a small city south of Florence that was popular with artists during the Renaissance, and despite his impressive international portfolio, he still resides there in a complex of ancient buildings that have been transformed into a singular home.

Baciocchi brought a world of colour and life to the once-decrepit buildings. After faithfully restoring the original *cocciopesto* plaster walls (in which earthenware and brick are combined with the usual lime and sand), he animated them with abstract, colour-blocked murals – a contemporary foil to the structure's original eighteenth-century frescos. The furniture is a mix of heavy wooden antiques, gallery-worthy mid-century pieces from coveted designers such as Gio Ponti, and comforta-ble sofas upholstered in vibrant hues. Perhaps the property's most striking feature, however, is the way Baciocchi has been able to highlight the patina of age, treating the marks of history as if they were precious artworks themselves.

A soulful restoration where the walls became a canvas

A soulful restoration where the walls became a canvas

1 A vintage chair by Gio Ponti sits next to the stone stairwell, which is lined with kitsch figurines. 2 A Murano glass Poliedri chandelier by Venini hangs from the original wooden rafters. 3 There is a passageway hidden behind what appears to be an armoire door. 4 Modern furniture in bold primary colours contrasts with the cloudy *cocciopesto* plaster walls. 5 The ancient building is a labyrinth of connecting rooms. 6 Baciocchi asked an artist friend to paint abstract fields of colour on the walls.

A futuristic subterranean island dwelling

Ventotene, Lazio
Francesca Amfitheatrof

The island of Ventotene, a two-hour ferry ride across the Tyrrhenian Sea from the port of Naples, sits within a sparse archipelago known as the Isole Pontine (Pontine Islands). The remnants of a now-dormant volcano, this island once hosted the summer residence of Roman Emperor Augustus, and the remains of his palatial villa can still be found overlooking the rocky coast.

Francesca Amfitheatrof, artistic director of jewellery and watches at Louis Vuitton, spent her childhood summers on Ventotene, swimming in the turquoise waters and exploring the island's scrubby hills. In 2012, after a long absence, she returned for a visit and found her own permanent retreat, in a context those unfamiliar with the region might consider unusual. Cave homes are a typical sight on these islands: the porous volcanic rock that forms the rugged outcrops is soft and easily carved, so for thousands of years the inhabitants of Ventotene built their homes into cliff faces, where they lived protected from the harsh winds of winter and summer's blazing heat.

After several years of painstaking restoration, Amfitheatrof has created a sophisticated and future-facing dwelling. The walls are finished with a glossy plaster, rendering the rough, raw stone smooth and white. The furniture is largely carved directly from the rock, save for a few rattan light fittings and soft, boulder-like armchairs. A 'C'-shaped kitchen island emerges from the centre of the floor like the control panel of a spaceship, while a sunken seating area has been excavated from the ground to form a cosy fireside nook. Light floods in from a glassed-in skylight above, making this subterranean space feel surprisingly airy, bright and welcoming.

A futuristic subterranean island dwelling

1 The sunken seating area and fireplace echo the natural curves of the cave. 2 Vintage rattan and bamboo chairs by Rohé Noordwolde in the outdoor living area. 3 Skylights filter sunlight in from above. 4 The main living area sports a 1970s rattan palm tree light by Mario Lopez Torres. 5 Even the kitchen countertop is curved.

A futuristic subterranean island dwelling

A minimalist apartment with a creative past

Rome
Serena Mignatti

Rome has always been a city of artists. From the artisans who tiled the ancient Roman villas and bathhouses with their elaborate mosaics to the Renaissance titans – artists such as Caravaggio, Michelangelo and Gian Lorenzo Bernini – poets, writers, musicians and actors have flocked to this living museum for generations. Some, as it happens, have even wound up sharing the same address.

In the 1980s, celebrated novelist Italo Calvino – author of the novels *The Baron in the Trees* (1957) and *Invisible Cities* (1972) – called this rooftop apartment in the Campo Marzio district home. Today it is the creative retreat of musician Thom Yorke of Radiohead and the actress Dajana Roncione. After purchasing the property from Calvino's daughter, the couple tasked Roman architect Serena Mignatti with breathing new life into the nineteenth-century penthouse, which had been left largely unchanged since Calvino lived there decades before.

Mignatti devised a serene, almost monastic space, characterized by natural materials, earth tones and organic forms. Cloudy, limewashed walls, a swirling solid oak staircase and vaulted ceilings that recall the architecture of Roman baths strike a modern contrast with the original wooden beams and exposed brick walls. Also left untouched was Calvino's library, where the author spent his days reading and writing. It was preserved almost as he had left it, as a thoughtful tribute to the home's artistic soul.

A minimalist apartment with a creative past

1 A Ciotola Maxi light fitting by Renzo Serafini hangs above the reclaimed wood kitchen table. 2 The bathroom walls are finished with a cloudy terracotta-toned limewash. 3 The apartment features original wooden beams. 4 A contemporary curving, solid oak staircase connects the floors. 5 Antique wooden doors in the bedroom.

A minimalist apartment with a creative past

A fashion designer's idiosyncratic city apartment

Milan
Francesco Risso

When fashion designer Francesco Risso took on the role of creative director at Marni in 2016, he brought with him a penchant for vivid colours, clashing styles and a punkish, DIY-inspired edge; his Milanese apartment follows a similar ethos. Risso effectively dissolved any sense of the refined, Liberty-style palazzo's bourgeois propriety with his anarchic decorating methods: full-size murals and matching curtains are painted free-hand, a patchwork bedspread resembling Neanderthal garb is strewn across a bamboo bed, and the hanging vines and spindly cacti scattered around the house call to mind an untamed jungle.

Amidst the madness, however, there is order. Risso's spectacular collection of contemporary and twentieth-century design speaks to his excellent taste and keen eye. In the kitchen, an almost cartoonish two-dimensional dining set designed in the 1960s by Anders Berglund and Hans Johansson, sits in contrast to the ascetic white-tile walls and clusters of vibrant green plants. Meanwhile, in the living room, eccentric hand-scrawled wall paintings and a patterned coffee table by the London-based designer Martino Gamper lend a contemporary edge to the vintage De Sede leather sofas, imposing marble fireplace and wooden marquetry floors.

A fashion designer's idiosyncratic city apartment

1 A jungle of hanging plants trails above a dining set by Anders Berglund and Hans Johansson. 2 In the master bedroom a bamboo bed and mirror by Gabriella Crespi are set against painted walls depicting galloping horses and tromp l'oeil frames. 3 A playful tiger bedspread in the guest bedroom. 4 The sitting room features a shearling Viggo Boesen armchair and a 1968 sofa by Jørgen Hø. 5 A vintage de Sede sofa and Martino Gamper coffee table in the living room.

A fashion designer's idiosyncratic city apartment

A celebrated designer's secret pied-à-terre

Turin
Carlo Mollino

When the polymath Carlo Mollino died in 1973, he left behind a wealth of secrets. An enlightened and passionate architect and designer, a brilliant engineer, and even an accomplished pilot and race-car driver, he was best known for his technically advanced yet subtly organic furniture and magnificently appointed buildings. Behind closed doors, however, Mollino pursued a host of esoteric interests – mostly here, in his secret apartment on Turin's Via Napione. For decades the apartment remained Mollino's private retreat, its existence unknown to many of his closest friends.

Overlooking the River Po, this was a place where he could discretely act out his fantasies (a trove of his erotic photography was discovered here after his death). He never lived in it, and apparently never even stayed the night. Instead, he treated – and furnished – the flat as if it were his own personal shrine. One theory is that it was designed to resemble a pharaoh's tomb. An Egyptologist from Turin's

Egyptian Museum came to visit the home following its transformation into a museum in 1999 and decreed that the butterfly imagery, draped animal skins and boat-like bed atop a sea of blue carpet (the ancient Egyptians believed souls travelled on boats to the afterlife) were all references to ancient funerary rites, purposefully arranged to ferry Mollino himself to the afterlife when his time came. The home's vast cache of treasures and decadent styling do indeed call to mind the spoils unearthed within the great pyramids.

Whether or not that is the case, Casa Mollino remains among the Turinese architect's most fantastic creations, and one of the greatest of the mysteries he left behind.

1 The dining room features a set of Eero Saarinen Tulip chairs and a marble table with legs resembling Ancient Greek columns. 2 The home's entranceway. 3 The sitting room juxtaposes a chaise lounge by Charlotte Perriand and Le Corbusier with giant clam shells and a zebra hide carpet. 4 Elaborately patterned tiles line the floor and walls of the bathroom.

A celebrated designer's secret pied-à-terre

A design curator's gallery-like home

Milan
Nicolas Bellavance-Lecompte

The Cinque Vie neighbourhood in the historic centre of Milan forms the ancient nucleus around which the city expands in concentric circles. It was the site of the first Roman settlements in the region, and vestiges of ancient churches and villas are still visible in the crumbling ruins scattered through the neighbourhood's backstreets. Most of the buildings that stand today were constructed around the sixteenth century, but many of those were heavily damaged during the bombing of World War II. In their place, modernist buildings emerged, creating a diverse and architecturally mixed neighbourhood.

The gallerist and architect Nicolas Bellavance-Lecompte moved into his spacious apartment here in 2018. The building, a former convent built in the early twentieth century, was bombed and rebuilt after World War II, like many of its neighbours. The flat was originally organized as a succession of small, cloistered rooms, which have been combined to create a series of open spaces that can accommodate large gatherings.

A long-time champion of contemporary design, Bellavance-Lecompte is the co-founder of Carwan Gallery and the biannual design fair Nomad, so naturally, his apartment is teeming with pieces by the designers with whom he has collaborated over the years. In the office, a looping brass chandelier by Paul Matter hangs above a desk by Oeuffice, Bellavance-Lecompte's own design brand. In the bedroom stands an elastic and aluminium bed by Belgian designer Bram Kerkhofs. A handwoven wool tapestry by the Iranian artist Taher Asad-Bakhtiari is mounted on a wall in the dining room, adjacent to a pair of vibrant red chairs by Palestinian brand Local Industries.

Like the neighbourhood that surrounds it, Bellavance-Lecompte's apartment encapsulates Milan's dynamic blend of ancient heritage and modern vibrancy.

1 A twisting brass chandelier by Paul Matter hangs above an Oeuffice desk in the office.
2 There is a portrait of Bellavance-Lecompte by Giovanni De Francesco in the kitchen.
3 In the main living space, Moulin Chairs by Pierre Paulin are arranged around a marble table by Oeuffice.

A renovation project where minimalism meets opulence

Naples
Klaus Schuwerk

Palazzo Carignani di Novoli is a sixteenth-century palace in the historic centre of Naples. Once the home of the noble Carignani di Novoli clan, it looks out over Piazza del Plebiscito, the city's largest and most central piazza. When German architect Klaus Schuwerk, best known for designing the National Museum in Oslo with his studio Kleihues + Schuwerk, found what is now his nine-room apartment on the palazzo's first floor, it had been abandoned for decades. Enamoured by its exquisite original features and sweeping views over the city, he took on the task of restoring the apartment and updating it for modern life.

The Neapolitan aesthetic sensibility has always been attuned to the extravagant, and this house is no different. Each of the home's doorways is decorated like a grand portal: sky blue illustrations with gilded edging surround the entrances to the bedroom; in the living room, the soaring balcony doors are framed by intricately embroidered silk and velvet panels; in the dining room, botanical motifs appear on blackened carved wood. Schuwerk balanced the opulence with bare white walls and minimal furnishings. Bent aluminium Thonet chairs and a sleek marble and glass table – made from a piece of stone salvaged from the National Museum facade – give the dining room's more lavish elements room to breathe.

Schuwerk pulled threads from the historical tapestry of Naples and interpreted them in details like the blackened wood shelving in the library, which echoes the material of the elaborately carved fireplace and doorframes. On a minimal bedside table sits a green glass amphora once used to catch octopi, a small yet evocative reminder of the city's rich history.

1 Hand-decorated velvet and silk panels border the living room doorway. 2 The apartment looks over Piazza del Plebiscito, the city's largest square. 3 The bedroom is adorned with 18th-century Neopolitan tile floors and hand-painted doorframes. 4 Blackened wood shelves and 19th-century *cementine* tiles in the library.

A renovation project where minimalism meets opulence

A creative couple's cabinet of curiosities

Milan
Andrea Zanatelli
& Kenny Spooren

A complaint one often hears about Milan is that the city operates behind closed doors. Usually the sentiment refers to its culture of exclusivity, but it also rings true in the literal sense: Milan is home to a disproportionate population of collectors and aesthetes, who pour their passions and accumulated treasures into private domains. Among them are Andrea Zanatelli, an artist, and Kenny Spooren, a communications manager, whose apartment in a 1960s building in the working-class neighbourhood of Giambellino is a veritable treasure trove.

Inside, the two-bedroom apartment boasts an aesthetic more akin to an eclectic Victorian manor than a modern-day flat. In fact, the couple point to several stately English homes as sources of inspiration – like the Bloomsbury Group's Charleston and Vita Sackville-West's Sissinghurst Castle. A constant north star for the couple is the work of William Morris, an early proponent of the nineteenth-century Arts and Crafts movement.

Since moving into the flat in 2018, Zanatelli and Spooren have been trawling Italy's auction houses and antique markets, searching for objects with an existing patina. Crossing the home's threshold from the strip-lit apartment hallway, visitors are plunged into an atmosphere of romantic antiquity. Immediately next to the door lives a console decorated with Grecian friezes, bought in Turin. On top sit plaster busts by a Belgian sculptor, as well as an antique Chinese ceramic candle holder and a pair of wooden candlesticks from a baroque Italian church. In the living room, an assemblage of mid-century furniture sits next to a faux-marble cabinet, where the anachronistic modern television is hidden behind the glass.

Fabrics form the bedrock of Zanatelli and Spooren's collection. Indonesian *ikats*, Uzbekistani *suzani* and Ottoman and Chinese silks are set into frames or draped on the walls and furniture, and Victorian needlework covers pillows and a collection of footstools once used by nuns in convent workshops.

A creative couple's cabinet of curiosities

A creative couple's cabinet of curiosities

1 An assortment of fabrics and Kilim cushions cover a vintage sofa by Martin Visser for Spectrum. 2 The floral decoration of the Piedmontese chest of drawers was likely added by a travelling artist who specialized in upgrading simple countryside furniture. 3 The couple created a headboard from an old Kilim rug. 4 The entranceway is lined with all manner of objects from different dates and origins. 5 A Pablo Bronstein print (top right) hangs on the living room bookcase – one of the few pieces of contemporary art in the apartment. 6 On a plate rack in the kitchen there is a collection of Staffordshire flatback figurines and John Derian plates by Astier de Villatte.

An elegantly layered island retreat

Capri, Campania
Studio Peregalli

Ever since the 1960s, Italian celebrities and Hollywood stars have convened every summer on the island of Capri, a jewel in the Gulf of Naples, to see, be seen, and frolic amid the waves. But Capri also has a quieter side. Far from the buzzing Piazzetta, the rugged landscape is verdant with Mediterranean plant life. And even though superyachts swarm the turquoise waters and streams of tourists pour from the daily ferries every July and August, Capri remains a place of escape.

Escape was the objective of architects Laura Sartori Rimini and Roberto Peregalli when it came to this holiday home. The pair are the masterminds behind Studio Peregalli, the renowned Milan-based interior design firm, famed for their incredible ability to evoke the past.

The structure was built in the 1950s by a Danish transplant who ran a well-known bar in town. Small, simple and entirely nondescript, the home's charms lie in its surroundings. The property is sheltered by a rocky cliff face and shaded by leafy

palms and ancient olive trees. Studio Peregalli's intervention transformed the plain white box into a richly layered retreat inspired by the island's extravagant historic villas.

Known for repurposing heirloom materials, Rimini and Peregalli found a trove of old Neapolitan tiles at an antiques fair and plastered them, quilt-like, across the floors and walls. They washed other walls with bright, patinated colours and furnished the house with charming antiques and resplendent textiles. The home now feels as if it were excavated from a Victorian novel, conjuring the sensation of an exquisite imaginary past.

1 In front of the window there is a Regency-era French desk and two fifteenth-century marble busts sit on the mantelpiece. 2 The verdant grounds are landscaped around an ancient olive tree. 3 Patterned tiles from the 19th century line the floor and walls. 4 Antique textiles in one of the home's three bedrooms.

An elegantly layered island retreat

A rural estate that celebrates art and craft

Val di Noto, Sicily
Riccardo Priolisi
& John Hooks

The towns and villages in Sicily's southeastern Val di Noto region are famous for their UNESCO-protected baroque buildings rendered in sand-coloured limestone; they are often described as open-air sculpture parks. Val di Noto's hinterlands, on the other hand, are mostly scrubby and wild, with arid hills and deep ravines. It was here that Riccardo Priolisi and John Hooks, an Italian–British couple previously employed in Italy's fashion industry, found their personal refuge in a long-abandoned *masseria* – a traditional agricultural complex – built in 1860. Over the span of three years, Priolisi and Hooks transformed the crumbling rural outpost into a grand estate that reflects their passions for modernist art and Classical culture.

To enter the property, known as Masseria Cardinale, one must pass through an arched gate set into the wall beneath a defensive turret designed to keep out the roving gangs of brigands who stalked this remote terrain in the nineteenth century. A wide central courtyard sits just inside, bordered by short buildings adorned with elaborate detailing. In designing the space, Priolisi, who spearheaded the scheme himself, married the *masseria's* original architecture with his own sophisticated style. In the living room – originally the farm's grain store – he painted the expansive walls with lounging figures inspired by Pablo Picasso's drawings. The floors are laid with handmade *cotto* tiles and local stone in a traditional Sicilian chevron pattern, while the ceilings are composed of *cane intrecciato* (woven rattan).

Thoughtful details abound in the house. In a sitting room, an Indian block-printed fabric is draped on the walls. Rows upon rows of eighteenth-century architectural engravings hang in the morning room and the kitchen's original octagonal stove has been restored with hand-painted majolica tiles. An oasis in the heart of the rugged Val di Noto, Masseria Cardinale stands as a testament to the harmonious blend of history, artistry and personal vision.

A rural estate that celebrates art and craft

A rural estate that celebrates art and craft

1 Masseria Cardinale was originally a farming hamlet with a series of stone courtyards. 2 The couple transformed the former stable into a dining room. 3 Priolisi replicated figures from Picasso's drawings of Ovid's *Metamorphoses* on the living room walls. 4 The library is filled with classic books and vintage furniture. 5 The octagonal pouffe was reupholstered in red and white Toile de Jouy fabric. 6 An antique folding chair in the living room.

An artist's rustic farmhouse that became her canvas

Siena, Tuscany
Maro Gorky

Think of Tuscany, and chances are you will picture quaint stone farmhouses with exposed wooden beams and deep marble sinks, surrounded by rolling hills of grapevines and towering rows of cypress trees. This rustic property half an hour's drive north of Siena certainly fits the stereotype – at least from the outside.

When the artist Maro Gorky, daughter of renowned Abstract Expressionist Arshile Gorky, and her husband, sculptor and writer Matthew Spender, purchased the abandoned farmhouse in 1968, animals were living in the property. Over the years, Gorky and Spender painstakingly restored the residence inch by inch, turning it into a haven in which to raise their family and nurture their creative tribe. Throngs of art-world luminaries have passed through the doors, and, in fact, the house is said to be the inspiration for Bernardo Bertolucci's 1996 film *Stealing Beauty*, which centres on an artist colony in the Tuscan countryside. Most importantly, the home has become Gorky's canvas. Each room has

been transformed into a living artwork. The dynamic murals Gorky has splashed across the walls mimic the vistas framed by the farmhouse's windows, resulting in a captivating play of perspective between the artist's handiwork and the landscape beyond.

An artist's rustic farmhouse that became her canvas

1 The crumbling farmhouse was being used to house animals when Maro Gorky bought it in the 1960s. 2 Paintings and photographs accumulated over the last 60 years line the walls. 3 Gorky hand-painted vibrant frescoes inspired by the Tuscan landscape on the walls of the farmhouse. 4 The impressive collection of glassware and ceramics in the dining room. 5 The wood-lined library.

An artist's rustic farmhouse that became her canvas

A visionary architect's hilltop sanctuary

Bocca di Magra, Liguria
Luisa Castiglioni, Maddalena Scarzella
& Matteo Petrucci

In the 1950s, Bocca di Magra – a small fishing village at the mouth of the Magra River, near the border between Liguria and Tuscany – was a magnet for intellectuals of the day. Luminaries such as Italo Calvino and Pier Paolo Pasolini were known to frequent the town in the summer months, drawn by the rugged landscape and simple way of life. These figures formed the Società degli Amici di Bocca di Magra, a group dedicated to preserving the charm and authenticity of the region. Among them was the architect and designer Luisa Castiglioni. Near the end of the decade, she was invited by a resident to design a holiday home for his family. It wasn't long before Castiglioni decided to build a similar house for herself.

Over two decades Castiglioni built three houses on a wooded hill between Bocca di Magra and Montemarcello. She split her time between Bocca di Magra and Milan until her death in 2015, when the property was passed down to her granddaughter, Maddalena Scarzella, and her partner, Matteo Petrucci, who are both architects. The couple have restored the property in line with Castiglioni's original vision, giving it the name 'Boccamonte'.

While all unique, the three houses follow a cohesive ethos of modernist functionality. Large windows look out towards the Apuan Alps and the Magra in the distance. Staggered volumes within the house play with perspective, leaving ample room for collections of objects and books. Much of the furniture is of Castiglioni's own design: a simple teak dining table, floating book-cases and a cleverly wrought desk that folds into the wall. Elsewhere, an eclectic array of artefacts and mementoes accumulated from a life of travels. African masks, ceramics from China and Turkish Kilim rugs add a cultural richness to the space, continuing the Bocca di Magra legacy of intellectual curiosity.

A visionary architect's hilltop sanctuary

1 A pair of lacquered wood armchairs by Umberto Riva and a Luminator floor lamp by Achille & Pier Giacomo Castiglioni in the living room. 2 Staggered steps lead to a built-in bench in the dining area. 3 A Franco Albini rattan ottoman and kilim rug in one of the sitting rooms. 4 One of the bedrooms boasts a bentwood Thonet armchair. 5 Expansive windows overlook the wooded hillside. 6 A Wassily chair by Marcel Breuer sits next to a wicker rocking chair.

A visionary architect's hilltop sanctuary

A radical designer's whimsical mountain house

Olda, Bergamo
Alessandro Mendini

Milanese designer, architect and editor Alessandro Mendini was a key player in the Italian postmodern and Radical Design movements. His colourful, often whimsical designs drew from influences as diverse as modern philosophy, antique furniture and ancient cultures, and he worked prolifically and consistently from the 1960s until his death in 2019.

The designer's mountain house in the town of Olda channels his unique sensibility. Situated in the Italian Alps, two hours south of the Swiss border, the Art Nouveau-style chalet stands out like an iced gingerbread house against the alpine landscape. Inside, Mendini painted the walls in bright pastel colours – a calling card of his own designs – which play against the elaborately carved cornices, patterned tiles and frescoed ceilings.

He furnished the home as if it were an informal gallery for his own creations: an oversized colour-blocked vessel named after the eighteenth-century thinkers Denis Diderot and Jean-Jacques Rousseau stands watch over the doorway; a collage-like side-board balances on a pedestal in the bedroom; and rugs woven with his bombastic illustrations function like canvases strewn across the floor.

However, it is one of his most iconic pieces, the Proust Chair – a baroque-style throne draped in fields of vibrant colour – that largely dictates the aesthetic throughout. The pointillist decoration of the original pops up as a recurring theme, replicated on beds, mirrors, carpets and tables, infusing the space with a technicolour dynamism only Mendini could have authored.

A radical designer's whimsical mountain house

A radical designer's whimsical mountain house

1 In the entranceway there is a pendant light by Hopf & Wortmann and a colourful vase of Mendini's own design. 2 One of the guest rooms features a cabinet he designed in 2007. 3 An array of Mendini's colourful designs in the playroom. 4 Speckled furniture in the living room nods to his iconic Proust chair. 5 The bedroom windows look out across the surrounding mountains. 6 Another colourful cabinet designed by Mendini.

A storied castle given a second life

Montespertoli, Tuscany
Baron Alessandro de Renzis Sonnino
& Baroness Caterina de Renzis

When Baroness Caterina de Renzis and her late husband Baron Alessandro de Renzis Sonnino inherited Castello Sonnino from a distant relative in 1988, it was a shell of its magnificent former self. The castle sat at the heart of a 370-acre (150-hectare) farm that produced wine and olive oil, but the structure had been largely abandoned for decades. The building's foundations were laid in the thirteenth century but the majority of the house was built later on, in the sixteenth century. Previous owners boasted important family names like Machiavelli and Strozzi. Still, its most historically significant period was the early 1900s, when it was used as a countryside home by the two-time Italian prime minister Sidney Sonnino.

Faced with such a decadent and storied past, the couple took on the task of revitalising Castello Sonnino. They moved in with their two young children and spent the following years bringing it back to life. They spruced up the antique furniture, refinished the crumbling surfaces and touched up the elaborate frescos that dance across the walls and ceilings, making them newly vibrant and crisp. The most stunning among these, in the living room, is a finely detailed illustration depicting a panoramic landscape; here, weeping willows, fruit trees and roses climb across all four walls and the vaulted ceiling, adding a sense of whimsy to the otherwise imposing manse. Now the castle plays many roles: as a home, a working farm, and an educational centre for visiting students to learn about Tuscany's history and local agriculture.

A storied castle given a second life

A storied castle given a second life

1 Hunting trophies in one of the home's sitting rooms. 2 A collection of antique and modern paintings. 3 Family photographs and an antique rocking chair. 4 The castle's study holds the archives of former Italian prime minister Sidney Sonnino. 5 The sixteenth-century castle was full of antiques when the de Renzis family inherited it. 6 Detailed frescoes in the main living room.

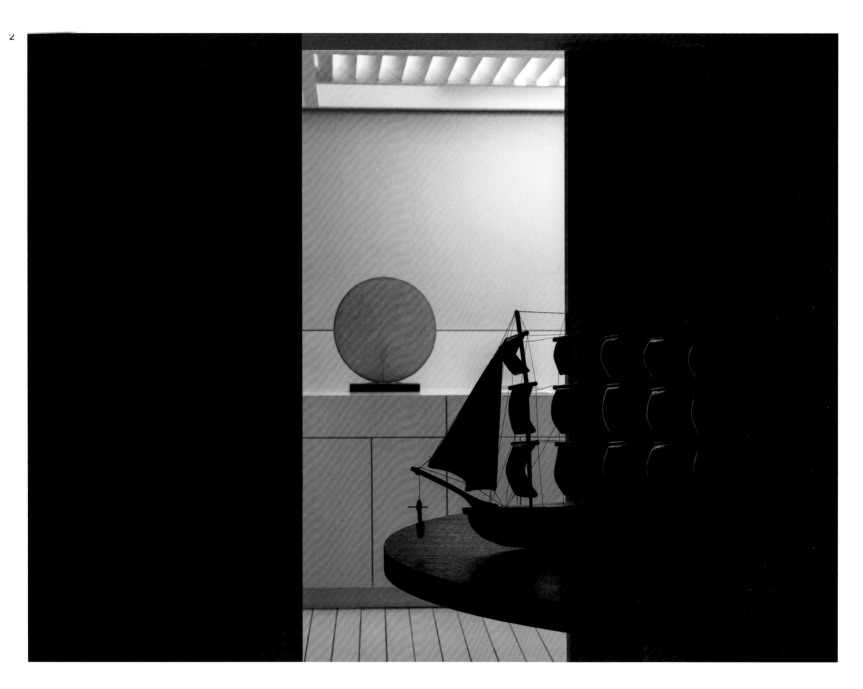

An iconic designer's remote island getaway

Pantelleria, Sicily
Giorgio Armani

Since 1975, the renowned Milanese designer Giorgio Armani has built a fashion empire with his timeless tailoring and ethereal red-carpet gowns. Less documented is his long-standing passion for interior design. In addition to creating furniture for his own high-end brand, he has been the primary creative force behind the constellation of elegantly appointed holiday homes he owns, scattered across the globe. They share the style and rigour of his eponymous brand.

Armani purchased this property on windswept Pantelleria in 1981, long before the island became a buzzing tourist destination. A remote and rocky outcrop halfway between Sicily and Tunisia, its landscape is defined by black volcanic stone that tumbles into the Mediterranean. Armani's getaway comprises a series of traditional *dammusi* – short, roughly made lava-stone homes crowned with domed roofs – in a small inlet known as Cala Gadir. In renovating the complex, he introduced natural materials that blend with the landscape, painted the walls in soothing shades of taupe and pale blue, and organized the layout in a way that allows him to live seamlessly between the indoors and out. Ultimately, the result is a space that beautifully merges Armani's own refined aesthetic with the island's wild soul.

1 The home's main sitting room. 2 The neutral colours throughout reflect the sun-bleached surroundings. 3 The space is furnished with a mix of modern furniture and antiques. 4 One of several bedrooms in the holiday home.

An iconic designer's remote island getaway

Pantelleria, Sicily

A former workshop turned artistic den

Milan
Roberto Gerosa

Milan may be best known for its aristocratic *palazzi* and striking modernist edifices, but it is also, perhaps most importantly, a working city. Threaded through residential neighbourhoods are small workshops and factories, where woodworkers, ceramicists, glassmakers and other artisans produce their wares. As cities change and evolve, these industrial spaces often become homes for artists, who inevitably put their own creative stamp on them.

Roberto Gerosa, an artist, architect and designer, moved into this former wood workshop in 2020. A magpie collector, he has populated the home with fanciful objects accumulated from a lifetime of art directing for brands and restoring historic homes. Most of the furniture he either designed himself – a brown suede sofa with swivelling sections on either side, several sets of wooden shelves, and the robin's-egg blue drawers in his bedroom, which allow all of their contents to be observed at once – or found by scouring antiques

fairs in Italy, France and Spain. Among these treasures is a heavy brass bed that was imported from India. It sits beneath a wall artfully cluttered with found photographs purchased at markets in Florence, where Gerosa went to school and lived for many years. Early in his career Gerosa also worked as a set designer for independent films, and that theatrical sensibility remains, most notably in the tromp l'oeil paper columns, once used as stage backgrounds, that adorn the concrete walls.

In addition to his work as a restorer, Gerosa designs bespoke lamps. His creations illuminate the space from all corners: a circular brass pendant hangs above the kitchen island, itself custom-made from a wooden door left by the previous tenant; a small cloud-like sconce, carved from translucent alabaster sourced from Volterra in Tuscany, is affixed high on a structural column; and all around stars, moons and suns – hand-crafted celestial bodies – descend from the ceiling.

1 Gerosa designed swivelling cushions on this suede sofa. 2 The kitchen island was made from a door left behind by the previous tenant. 3 Gerosa's bedroom, where he keeps his extensive collection of books. 4 The antique brass bed is from India.

A former workshop turned artistic den

A 13th-century castle brought back to life by a master of illusion

Cigognola, Lombardy
Renzo Mongiardino

The decorator and set designer Renzo Mongiardino holds a rarefied place among interior designers. The homes he created for aristocrats and celebrities – such as Gianni Versace, the Onassis family and the Rothschilds – remain some of the most revered and highly coveted in the twentieth-century canon. His spaces were conceived to evoke wonder and suspend disbelief, transporting their occupants into another, more fantastical world.

Perched atop the crest of a hill in the Oltrepò Pavese, about an hour south of Milan, Castello di Cigognola was originally built as a defensive watchtower in the thirteenth century, but over the centuries it was significantly expanded, resulting in the sprawling complex that exists today. In the 1980s, following a devastating fire, the Moratti family, which has owned the property for generations, was faced with the prospect of restoring their ancestral home. Mongiardino was a long-time family friend; he had worked with the clan on their charity,

Comunità di San Patrignano, which teaches craft skills to recovering addicts. He was the natural choice to bring the stately home back to life.

When Mongiardino unleashed his vision on the house, each room became a kaleidoscopic maelstrom of print, texture and colour. As an accomplished set designer – he was nominated for two Academy Awards – he utilized every available trompe l'oeil trick of the stage. Wooden panels are carefully painted to look like fabric, while what appear to be marble slabs on the walls are actually wallpaper. Everything is elaborate, but nothing is as it seems. A dizzying array of patterns saturates each room: from hand-stencilled motifs that wind up the walls and along coffered ceilings to the prim bedrooms' matching comforters, wallpaper and even lampshades, like a chintz take on camouflage. Even now, thirty years later, nearly everything is how Mongiardino left it – a living monument to the inimitable master.

A 13th-century castle brought back to life by a master of illusion

4

Cigognola, Lombardy

153

A 13th-century castle brought back to life by a master of illusion

1 A collection of antique busts sits atop a stone hearth in the sitting room. 2 A sculpture by the Polish artist Igor Mitoraj guards the home's grand entrance. 3 An imposing stone fireplace in what is known as the green room. 4 Delicate floral wallpaper lines the walls of one of the guest rooms. 5 In another guest bedroom, the wallpaper, bedspread and lamp all carry the same pattern. 6 Hand-stencilled patterns decorate the walls of the stairwell.

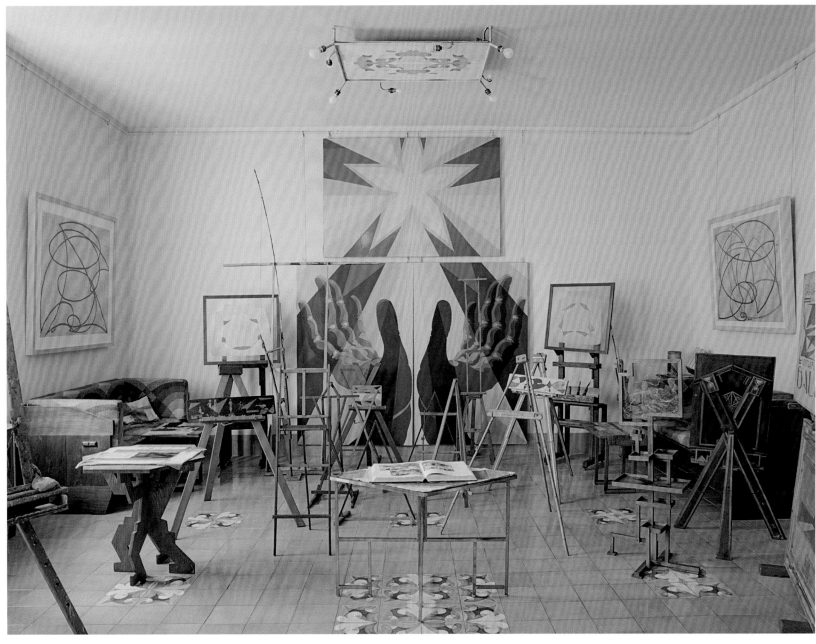

An expressive painter's home that became a work of art

Rome
Giacomo Balla

In the early twentieth century, a group of artists in Italy joined together to shape the future of art. They came up with 'The Futurist Manifesto', a document urging their contemporaries to embrace modernity and reject old-fashioned ways of thinking. Amongst the signees was Giacomo Balla, an artist known for dynamic paintings that introduced movement into static imagery, who would become one of the most influential figures of the period.

As an artist with such strong views, it is perhaps no surprise that his home was similarly extreme. His apartment on the northern peripheries of Rome represents a Gesamtkunstwerk – a total work of art. Over the thirty years he lived there with his wife and two daughters, Balla slowly transformed the simple worker's flat into a living canvas; he painted the walls, ceiling, furniture – practically everything – with his pastel fields of floating colour. Even the dishes in the kitchen and linens on the beds are his design.

Miraculously, the apartment has remained intact long after even his daughters, who also lived there their entire lives, passed away in the 1990s. Casa Balla, which is run by MAXXI – the National Museum of 21st Century Art – can be visited by appointment, and exists as a time capsule of one of Italy's most fruitful and significant artistic periods, as well as a testament to how the simple act of living can be a work of art in itself.

1 Colourful, hand-painted walls in the hallway. 2 Paintings by Balla and a collection of handmade easels in the living room. 3 Most of the furniture and furnishings were either customised or made by Balla. 4 Colourful chairs and futurist-style ceramics in the kitchen.

An expressive painter's home that became a work of art

A monastic home in the heart of an ancient village

Soleto, Puglia
Andrew Trotter
& Marcelo Martínez

Sunny, (relatively) flat and surrounded by the sparkling Mediterranean, Puglia – the heel of Italy's boot – feels a world away from the dense Italian metropolises of Rome or Milan. The sparsely populated and largely agricultural region is dotted with gnarly olive trees, blossoming almond groves and every type of citrus fruit tree, its gently rolling hills crowned with picturesque, whitewashed villages that resemble layered cakes baking in the sun. Unsurprisingly, the area has become a magnet for those seeking tranquillity and natural beauty, many of whom have become so enamoured with the place that they've decided to put down roots. Such is the case for architect Andrew Trotter and designer Marcelo Martínez, who have been breathing new life into Puglia's forgotten farmhouses and *palazzi* for several years.

Among their projects is Casa Soleto, a modest palazzo in the village of Soleto in the Salento region of Puglia. The home, it's believed, was first constructed nearly 400 years ago and many of its original features remain, including baroque details on the building's facade, worn terracotta floors and high, vaulted ceilings that keep the building cool and fresh through the blistering summers. In renovating the space, Trotter and Martínez restored it as faithfully as possible, while adding their own meditative sensibility to the design. Walls were limewashed in earthy shades of brown and left bare save for the occasional niche displaying handmade pottery or the odd thrifted painting. The sparse yet carefully considered furniture is a mix of antiques salvaged from a monastery and minimal, Scandinavian-inspired pieces – a balance of eras and perspectives that sit perfectly together in this beguiling retreat.

A monastic home in the heart of an ancient village

1 The traditional courtyard entrance of the home. 2 The main living room features a sofa by Blasco and a handwoven Mauritanian rug. 3 The vintage wooden furniture in the kitchen was left behind by the previous owners. 4 There is a plunge pool and seating area in the tranquil internal courtyard. 5 An original vaulted ceiling in one of the sitting rooms.

A monastic home in the heart of an ancient village

A modern family apartment in a historic palazzo

Genoa
Laura Garbarino

Palazzo Giustiniani is one of the so-called *Palazzi dei Rolli*, a unique cluster of privately owned palaces in a UNESCO-protected neighbourhood in the historic centre of Genoa. Built between the sixteenth and seventeenth centuries, these historic buildings were owned by powerful aristocratic families who were responsible for hosting distinguished individuals and state guests that visited the bustling port city. Prized for their extravagant decoration, they stand as enduring examples of Genoa's opulence during its prosperous mercantile era.

Laura Garbarino, an art expert at an auction house, her husband Luca Eleuteri and their three children made a home on the fourth floor of Palazzo Giustiniani, a jewel among the *Rolli*, in 2008. Built at the end of the sixteenth century, the palazzo's soaring 8-metre- (26-foot-) high ceilings are animated by elaborate frescos depicting mythological figures and valiant battles. Orders of gilded pilasters line the walls and, underfoot, the floors boast

intricate *terrazzo* or elaborate marquetry, showcasing spectacular craftsmanship.

In decorating the apartment, Gabarino, a passionate collector of contemporary art and vintage furniture, artfully balanced the surrounding drama with eclectic modern furnishings. From prized mid-century pieces such as a chaise-longue by Le Corbusier in the living room to arty contemporary pieces, including a collage-like chair by Martino Gamper, she has created a captivating fusion of the past and the present within the palatial setting.

A modern family apartment in a historic palazzo

1 The bedroom features a lamp by Gaetano Sciolari for Stilnovo, a 19th-century *dormeuse* and a sculpture by Claire Barclay. 2 Martino Gamper's 2008 Bird House chair. 3 The lighting was custom-designed by Davide Groppi. 4 A painting by artist Emmanuelle Antille hangs on the kitchen wall. 5 The textured wall of the bathroom is a ceramic finish designed by Tokujin Yoshioka for Mutina. 6 The living room features furniture inherited from Gabarino's grandmother and a painting by Ettore Spalletti.

A modern family apartment in a historic palazzo

A modernist pine-clad mountain house

Cortina d'Ampezzo, Veneto
Edoardo Gellner

In 1946 the Croatian architect Edoardo Gellner arrived in the northern Italian town of Cortina d'Ampezzo. He had just graduated from the faculty of architecture at the Università Iuav di Venezia and was settling down after the upheaval of World War II. Cortina d'Ampezzo was, and still is, primarily a tourist destination, catering to the ski resorts that feed into the village from the surrounding Dolomite mountains.

Gellner built Cà del Cembro, a five-story apartment building, in 1951 to house his own living space, his studio and several other apartments for friends and colleagues who had invested in the property. Traditionally, the region's mountain huts and chalets were composed of rough stone, with small windows and pitched wooden roofs. Gellner sought to marry that vernacular alpine style with modernist principles, doing away with the overbearing kitsch that often resulted from new interpretations of the local architecture.

Indeed, the interior of his apartment, which is still occupied by his niece, Eleonora, feels more akin to a ranch-style bungalow in California than a mountain hut. Gellner lined the walls in finely-grained pine, fashioned a sculptural hearth out of cast concrete and designed the windows to be as tall and as wide as possible to fully take in the impressive views of the mountains across the valley. A series of structures made of moulded ceramic bricks stamped with concentric circles seem to push through the walls, creating a sophisticated dialogue between inside and out.

A modernist pine-clad mountain house

1 A sculptural concrete fireplace in the sitting room. 2 The wood-lined walls make
a feature of the pine's natural grain. 3 The floorplan is set over a series of staggered
levels. 4 The apartment also functioned as Gellner's studio. 5 The balcony overlooks
the Dolomite mountain range. 6 A section of composed of moulded ceramic bricks
in the perimeter wall.

A modernist pine-clad mountain house

A stone townhouse filled with art and antiques

Giuggianello, Puglia
Peter Benson Miller
& Giovanni Panebianco

The small town of Giuggianello is located in the Salento region of Puglia. Historically prized for its strategic location along Mediterranean shipping routes, the area has long been a melting pot of cultures, blending influences from Greek, Roman, Byzantine and Ottoman civilizations. In 2014, art historian and curator Peter Benson Miller and his partner Giovanni Panebianco, a high-ranking civil servant, came across a quaint town-house with an expansive garden that had been abandoned for many years.

Likely built in fits and starts from the eighteenth century onwards, it was rich with architectural details typical of the region: *cementine* tile floors designed to resemble colourful woven carpets; high, star-vault ceilings; a facade made of local Pietra Leccese limestone; and decorative stone arches between the rooms. They restored the house with help from Roman design firm ma0, clearing away a warren of small rooms

to create an open space that flowed easily into the outdoors, where Miller has nurtured a Mediterranean garden of fruit trees, fragrant flowers and climbing roses.

Miller filled the home with contemporary works by the likes of Tomaso De Luca, Tristano di Robilant, Dawn Kasper and Leonid Lerman, while a custom-made stencil by young American artist F Taylor Colantonio encircles the wall of the guest room in place of wainscoting. Otherwise, objects and furnishings were inherited or discovered in markets and antique stores in Italy and abroad. A collection of nineteenth-century artist's palettes is scattered across the wall of a small sitting room. In the bedroom, religious paintings cluster around the headboard like a halo. The carved stone sinks were brought from Turkey, where they adorned a nineteenth-century hammam, embodying a cultural fusion reflective of this region's rich heritage.

1 The dining room features original *cementine* tile floors and Gothic arches. 2 A collection of antique religious iconography lines the bedroom wall. 3 The sculptural carved stone sink was sourced from a hammam in Turkey.

A stone townhouse filled with art and antiques

A sophisticated penthouse with a spectacular view

Rome
Alvisi Kirimoto

Few monuments encapsulate the magnificence of the Roman Empire better than the Colosseum. Still standing after some 2,000 years, it remains the nucleus around which modern Rome has grown. For those fortunate enough to live in its vicinity, organizing windows, terraces, balconies and any sliver of sightline towards it becomes a priority. It is almost as if the apartments and *palazzi* that have sprung up in its shadow over the centuries function as the final ring of seats in the amphitheatre.

That was essentially the brief given to Massimo Alvisi and Junko Kirimoto of Roman architecture firm Alvisi Kirimoto when they were commissioned to renovate this penthouse loft for an artist couple: to capitalize on the windows that overlook the city's terracotta roofs on all sides. Not wishing to compete with such an impressive scene, Alviso and Kirimoto conceived a rich yet simple palette of materials. There are chestnut-coloured wenge-wood parquet floors, glass doors lined with linen to let the natural

light penetrate, and bathroom sinks hewn from translucent onyx and rosy pink marble. Heavier materials are softened by the occasional swathe of wallpaper, printed with delicate floral motifs.

The choice of furniture also adds a sense of levity to the overall grandness of the design. According to the architects, the set of sofas by Gaetano Pesce – known for his colourful and often eccentric designs – are arranged on the raised platform in the centre of the attic floor to 'balance the monumentality of the historical context'.

A sophisticated penthouse with a spectacular view

A sophisticated penthouse with a spectacular view

1 A front-row view of the Colosseum from the rooftop terrace. 2 A collection of Gaetano Pesce sofas is arranged on a raised platform in the centre of the open-plan space. 3 The architects installed wraparound windows in the penthouse apartment. 4 The home's contemporary kitchen. 5 A Maarten Baas side table sits next to an antique wooden bed. 6 The bathroom features pale pink marble.

A painter's home and studio imbued with the patina of time

Trieste
David Dalla Venezia

The city of Trieste occupies a small sliver of land on the northeastern edge of Italy's Adriatic coast. Bordered by Slovenia on three sides, the region was part of the Austro-Hungarian Empire until the twentieth century, and the city has always existed at the intersection of Slavic and Italian cultures.

The painter David Dalla Venezia was born in Cannes but grew up in Venice. He found his Trieste home in 2016 – an apartment on an upper floor of the neoclassical Palazzo Panfilli. The palazzo, built between 1879 and 1881, sits within a neighbourhood of similar buildings known as Borgo Teresiano; the city-centre district was commissioned between the late eighteenth and mid-nineteenth centuries by the Austrian Empress Maria Theresa. When Dalla Venezia first came across the apartment, it had been abandoned for several years. The walls were painted dreary white and the wooden floor was grey with dust. After inspecting the sloppy renovation he discovered nineteenth-century wall decoration hidden beneath

the paint. He restored the palazzo by scraping the paint off the walls and then sanding and varnishing the solid oak floors and window frames. What was left was a stunning revelation of historical elegance mixed with the patina of time. The apartment now functions as his home and studio – a place he considers an extension of his artistic practice.

Most of the furniture was found in local flea markets and antique shops in Trieste, but some pieces came from his family's Venice home. These include a nineteenth-century walnut wardrobe that once belonged to his grandmother. His father, an artisan picture framer by trade, made the many wooden picture frames that adorn the house, as well as the dining table, chairs and bookshelves, which were built when Dalla Venezia lived in France as a boy. Elsewhere, the artist's collections of objects – tools, skulls, memorabilia, books – embellish the rooms, alongside his own captivating paintings and sculptures.

A painter's home and studio imbued with the patina of time

A painter's home and studio imbued with the patina of time

1 Antique wooden furniture in the rustic dining room. 2 The view through the apartment's enfilade of rooms. 3 Many of the picture frames found throughout the house were constructed by Dalla Venezia's father. 4 The apartment functions as both Dalla Venezia's home and workspace. 5 Art supplies, paintings and found objects in the home studio.

A frescoed palazzo with Roman foundations

Lucca, Tuscany
Cristiana Castagnetti

The town of Lucca – best known for the star-shaped defensive wall that encircles the historic centre of the town – is situated along the Serchio River in a low-lying valley between Florence and the Tyrrhenian coast. Vestiges of the original Roman city are still visible throughout the urban fabric. Palazzo Andriani, originally constructed in the sixteenth century, sits within a beautifully preserved historic neighbourhood (it is even said that the ruins found in the building's basement are the remains of the city wall's long-lost North Gate). The splendour of the structure as it stands now, however, can mostly be attributed to an eighteenth-century renovation, undertaken by the noble Andriani family.

The palazzo has functioned as the residence and embassy for the Spanish ambassador to the Duchy of Lucca, and, later on, as a tax office and bank. But when Elisabetta Pierallini and Giorgio Tenucci purchased a 500 m² (5,382 sq ft) slice of the palazzo in the late 2010s, it had been decrepit and abandoned

for several years. Restorations, made with the help of local architecture firm ReP Architetti, focused mainly on bringing back to life the palazzo's original features, like its detailed frescos. These trompe l'oeil columns, festooned curtains and dancing figures were added to from the seventeenth century onwards. In the living room, the illustrations reach six metres (twenty feet) skywards, towards the impressive vaulted ceiling.

Pierallini and Tenucci commissioned Cristiana Castagnetti, a designer from the Piedmontese city of Biella, to curate a selection of furniture that would complement the home's extravagant Renaissance aesthetic. The current decorations feature a mix of twentieth- and twenty-first-century finds: Pipistrello lamps by Gae Aulenti, an Ultrafragola mirror by Ettore Sottsass, 1970s Venini glass chandeliers, as well as jewel-toned, custom-made sofas that look as though they could have been plucked from a Regency-era manor – all adding another layer of history to this metic-ulously adorned palace.

A frescoed palazzo with Roman foundations

Lucca, Tuscany

1 Rattan-covered cupboard doors and a George Nelson pendant lamp by Herman Miller in the corridor. 2 The family's dachshund Pierino lounges on a Camaleonda sofa by Mario Bellini. 3 Dancing figures, mythical creatures and Corinthian pediments are painted as frescoes on the wall of the grand living room. 4 A white marble vanity adds a contemporary edge to the historic palazzo. 5 The home's breakfast room.

A frescoed palazzo with Roman foundations

An architect's industrial-style holiday home

Marina di Marittima, Puglia
Massimiliano Locatelli

The architect Massimiliano Locatelli made a name for himself by transforming unconventional spaces. His former office in Milan was based in a desecrated Renaissance church, where he constructed a floating glass-and-steel cube that elevated visitors to stand at eye level with the elaborate frescos painted on the ceiling. His holiday home in the Salento region of Puglia is similarly unorthodox. Rather than inserting industrial aesthetics into an ornamental context, he did the opposite. The low-slung building was once the office of a stone quarry. Now it is an austere yet inviting retreat furnished with mid-century design pieces, antiques imported from Southeast Asia and furniture designed by Locatelli himself.

Conceived as a space to host friends, Locatelli ironically describes the property as a 'luxury dormitory'. All of the eight bedrooms lining the long, 'L'-shaped structure have been reduced to essentials. Each is decorated identically, with an aluminium bed designed by Locatelli and a corresponding number

embroidered onto sheets and pillowcases. The ascetic environment is broken up, however, by colourful bedspreads handwoven in Vietnam.

Like the bedrooms, the rest of the house is dominated by stark metallic elements that shine against the grey-toned Lecce stone floors. In the kitchen, that meant stainless steel cabinets, a long black steel table and twelve die-cast aluminium chairs conceived by Locatelli. Just beyond the table, industrial sliding doors open into the courtyard, allowing indoor-outdoor living during the warm summer months – a prospect made even more appealing by the lavish rooftop pool that runs the length of the building.

An architect's industrial-style holiday home

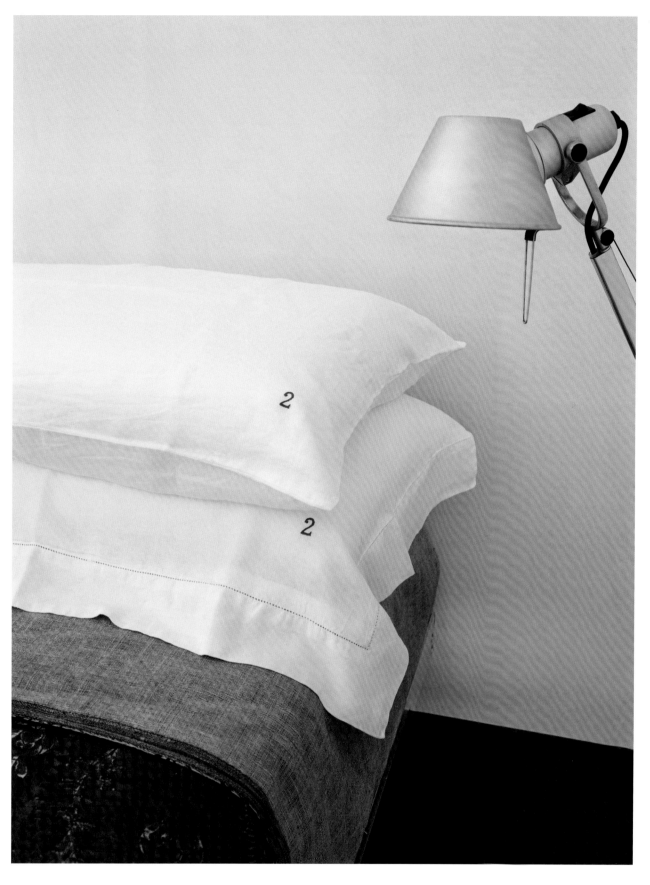

1 The matching guest rooms open onto the courtyard. 2 Puglia's weather makes it easy to merge indoor and outdoor living. 3 The kitchen features a four-metre-long black steel table and twelve die-cast aluminium chairs that Locatelli designed. 4 The corresponding room number is embroidered onto each guest room's pillow cases. 5 The aluminium beds were designed by Locatelli, while the bedspreads are from Vietnam.

An architect's industrial-style holiday home

Marina di Marittima, Puglia

An alpine homage to an architectural master

San Martino di Castrozza, Trentino
Bruno Morassutti

San Martino di Castrozza is a small alpine village best known as a seasonal resort; the population swells each winter with visitors arriving to enjoy the local ski slopes. It is perhaps somewhat surprising that here, among the pine trees, mountain peaks and kitschy chalets, is situated a homage to the modernist American architect Frank Lloyd Wright.

Following his graduation from Università Iuav di Venezia, the Padua-born architect Bruno Morassutti spent a period working and studying at Wright's Taliesin West architecture school and studio in Arizona. It was a formative period, one that would forever shape his oeuvre, which eventually included large-scale institutions and residential complexes. In 1956, when Morassutti set out to build his family home, here amid the Dolomite mountains, he endeavoured to integrate Wright's teachings.

Villa Morasutti sits precisely where the village gives way to a grassy meadow, and where the incline towards the Pale di San Martino mountain group

– the largest cluster of peaks in the entire Dolomite range – begins. Like Wright, who championed principles of organic architecture, Morassutti found beauty in natural materials like unpainted wood and local stone.

The latter forms the rough base of the home's most prominent and inviting feature, a floating fireplace that seemingly descends from a skylight in the centre of the living area. Each space flows easily into the next, punctuated by comfortable, built-in furniture and the occasional shock of red or royal blue. It is an inspired alpine interpretation of Wright's vision and legacy.

1 The glassed-in entranceway is a reference to Frank Lloyd Wright's ranch-style houses.
2 A low stone wall defines the perimeter of the living room. 3 A floating fireplace is the
centrepiece of the open-plan space.

An alpine homage to an architectural master

San Martino di Castrozza, Trentino

A contemporary apartment that goes against the grain

Venice
Marcante Testa

Designers often encounter a trap in Venice: the city is teeming with decoration – baroque, gothic, Byzantine, neoclassical and even modernist facades jostle for attention along the canals and around the *campi* (city squares). When tasked with envisioning a contemporary space in such an antique place, negotiating the historical precedents can become an aesthetic minefield. Remarkably, Andrea Marcante and Adelaide Testa of the Turin-based architecture and interior design firm Marcante Testa were able to free themselves from the city's ornamental abundance with their redesign of a nineteenth-century apartment in the central neighbourhood of San Marco.

Their name for the project, 'Another Venice', speaks to the desire to reimagine an aesthetic narrative. The architects concerned themselves with capturing the lagoon and its shifting colours in a way that didn't rely on kitsch or cliché. They did so by introducing contemporary materials and forms that fostered a fusion of ideas. In the living room, a series of folding panels is used in place of dividing walls to let natural light penetrate deep into the centre of the apartment. The structure is composed of painted metal and brass, while the inserts are formed of green glass or Venetian stucco, chosen to evoke the work of architect Carlo Scarpa (who was born in Venice and whose work was often inspired by the city).

Furniture by Scarpa and his architect son, Tobia, is found throughout the house. So are textiles from historic Venetian companies Rubelli and Fortuny. Metal frames climb through the bedroom and kitchen, creating a unifying logic throughout the house while introducing contrasting colours and materials. In a sitting room, Murano glass pendant lights hang from these suspended tracks, further reflecting the famous Venetian light as it shimmers off the canals.

A contemporary apartment that goes against the grain

A contemporary apartment that goes against the grain

1 A contemporary sideboard by Danish designer Finn Juhl in the entranceway.
2 The glass pendant lights by Nao Tamura in the dining room were inspired by
the colours of the Venetian lagoon. 3 The studio features a Leaf chandelier by MM
Lampadari and a Frate desk by Enzo Mari. 4 Digamma armchairs by Ignazio Gardella
and a Shimmer coffee table by Patricia Urquiola in the living room. 5 A ceramic totem
by Ettore Sottsass. 6 A custom mirrored wardrobe in the children's bedroom.

A countryside home for a creative family

Camaiore, Tuscany
Giovanni Pasanella
& Marco Pasanella

The northwest region of Lucca in Tuscany sits in a privileged position in the Italian peninsula. Sandwiched between the Apuan Alps, where snowy-white Carrara marble has been quarried for centuries, and the long, flat sandy beaches that border the Ligurian Sea, this idyllic slice of the country is teeming with attractions.

When the architect and academic Giovanni Pasanella purchased this eighteenth-century villa in the 1970s, the surrounding landscape became his muse. Populated by olive groves, fruit orchards and dense thickets of bushy pine trees, the hilltop property peers over the nearby town of Camaiore. In his retirement, Pasanella took to painting the panoramic vistas that unfurled around him, and evidence of his passion lives on in the home.

His son Marco and Marco's wife, Rebecca, have kept the elder Pasanella's spirit alive within the stone walls; from the watercolours hanging in the living room to old jars of paint pigments displayed in the former studio. Marco and Rebecca have not merely preserved the past, however; they have made the house their own, mixing sharp, contemporary furnishings with Tuscan antiques and vintage pieces designed by Giovanni, adding another chapter to the villa's intergenerational story.

1 Frescoes decorate the ceiling and stairwell in the entranceway. 2 Antique pieces
from Tuscany in the kitchen. 3 Stencilled floral motifs in the light-filled bedroom.
4 An antique wrought iron bed and wooden armoire.

A countryside home for a creative family

A reimagined brutalist masterpiece

Milan
Wannasiri Kongman
& Jesse Dorsey

The architect Vittoriano Viganò was a pioneer of Italian Brutalism. From the 1950s to the 1980s he designed a raft of buildings across Italy in the domineering modern style – most notably the faculty of architecture at the Politecnico di Milano university, as well as a select few private homes. When Jesse Dorsey and Wannasiri Kongman, the co-founders of accessories brand BOYY, were looking to relocate to Milan from their home in Bangkok, they were in the market for a place that tapped into the city's storied design history. Fortunately for them, that came in the form of a rare Viganò-designed home in the heart of the city's historic centre.

Viganò left his mark on the space – which spans the first two floors of a neoclassical building – in the 1970s, when the then-owner commissioned him to reimagine the apartment entrance, foyer, studio, living room and garden. When the couple first encountered the space, it hadn't been changed at all. The task they set for themselves was to preserve Viganò's brutalist interventions – the interlocking plaster panels that hang from the ceiling, the floating stone-and-cast-iron bridge that leads from the courtyard to the front door, and the steel superstructure extending from the facade – while modernizing the less comfortable aspects and introducing light.

Kongman and Dorsey incorporated design elements that purposefully engaged in dialogue with Viganò's design. Marble and bamboo wall panels now play against the home's shifting volumes, and stepping stone-like pieces of onyx inserted into the entranceway's concrete floor add a sense of levity. For furniture, they amassed an impressive collection of Italian design classics: a rattan armchair by Joe Colombo; a slender red loveseat by Gastone Rinaldi; reupholstered sofas and a dining room table by Viganò, in an homage to the legendary architect himself.

1 The view from the living room towards the private garden – a rarity in the centre of Milan. 2 The couple sourced a vintage dining table from the 1970s by Vittorio Viganò as an homage to the architect. 3 A Saturno sofa bench by Gastone Rinaldi in the entranceway. 4 Mirrored walls and onyx panels were added to the walls to bring a more playful touch to Viganò's brutalist volumes.

A reimagined brutalist masterpiece

A second-generation artist's countryside manor

Amelia, Umbria
Paolo Canevari

The region of Umbria – a landlocked province in the dead centre of Italy – is mostly rural. It is like Tuscany, but wilder, more remote and with considerable religious significance. Umbria is criss-crossed by the Via di Francesco (Saint Francis' Way), a pilgrimage trail that leads from La Verna, Tuscany, in the north and Rome to the south, with both routes meeting in Assisi, the place of Saint Francis's birth. But Umbria is also a place of escape – a short drive from Rome, it is a retreat for city dwellers during the scorching summers.

When the Roman artist Paolo Canevari's father, the late sculptor Angelo Enrico Canevari, found this patrician villa in 1980, it had long been abandoned by the previous owners, an aristocratic Roman family. Despite its state of degradation, its charms were intact. The elder Canevari spent the next few years slowly returning the house to its former splendour, leaving the structure untouched but sprucing up its frescos and redressing its rooms.

It wasn't until 2015, however – when Paolo returned to Italy from living abroad in the United States – that the younger Canevari made his mark on the space. He completely redesigned the first-floor apartment, filling it with objects he has collected throughout his life. He is enamoured with Art Nouveau furniture from the late nineteenth and early twentieth centuries; pieces by Carlo Bugatti, Louise Majorelle and Eugenio Quarti are scattered throughout the rooms. These are counter-balanced by modern designs from the 1950s and 1960s by the likes of Osvaldo Borsani, Pierre Paulin and Jacques Quinet.

The art is a slightly more personal affair. Drawings and sculptures by his grandfather and great-uncle live alongside Paolo's own work and coveted pieces by twenty-first-century art stars like Jannis Kounellis, Nam June Paik and James Lee Byars, whom Canevari also counts as friends.

1 Antique Japanese Bugaku masks line the walls of the upstairs sitting room. 2 An early twentieth-century wooden bed by Louis Majorelle and a painting by Henry Fehr in the bedroom. 3 A Tongue Chair by Pierre Paulin. 4 The sitting room features drawings by Paolo Canevari and Japanese *ukiyo-e* prints.

A second-generation artist's countryside manor

Amelia, Umbria

228

An ode to the city in a light-filled gothic palazzo

Venice
Paolo Castellarin
& Didier Bonnin

Venetian architecture is about as layered and complicated as the city itself. From the Middle Ages onwards the city was a hub of commerce and cultures, and the ebb and flow of people can still be read on its buildings' facades. Travellers returning from distant cities like Alexandria and Constantinople (now Istanbul) brought with them the influence of Islamic and Byzantine architecture – pointed *ogee* arches, patterned faces, decorative crenellations – which married with European architectural traditions to solidify into what is now known as the Venetian Gothic style.

Designer Paolo Castellarin and his husband Didier Bonnin found their own Venetian Gothic pied-à-terre in a fifteenth-century palazzo on the Rio Marin, a busy canal that runs along the border of the Santa Croce and San Polo districts. Set on the palazzo's *piano nobile* (typically the most ornately furnished floor), a row of four-metre-tall, arched marble windows dominate the living room,

peering over the adjacent canal. Light floods into the space and explodes against mirror-covered walls (mirrored rooms, known as *cabinets des glacés*, are common in Venice, a historic centre of glassmaking). Restored frescos above multiply in reflection, as if one were in a life-size kaleidoscope.

Castellarin populated the apartment with comparatively modern furnishings: a crystal Glas Italia sideboard by Piero Lissoni and a Vico Magistretti table in the dining room; a completely stainless steel kitchen; Marcel Breuer Wassily armchairs; a bulbous orange Naoto Fukasawa ottoman; a minimal, white Jean-Marie Massaud sofa; and a wheeled table by Gae Aulenti in the centre of the living room. Venice is the star of the dining room: mounted across the wall as if seen through a window, the Basilica of San Marco stands proud in a nineteenth-century chromolithograph by Ferdinando Ongania, thoughtfully connecting the floating city's past and present.

1 A nineteenth-century chromolithograph by Ferdinando Ongania in the dining room.
2 Mirrored rooms, known as *cabinets des glacés*, were a common feature of historic
Venetian *palazzi*. 3 The nineteenth-century panels in the bedroom depict a jungle
landscape. 4 A Nuage bookcase by Charlotte Perriand.

An ode to the city in a light-filled gothic palazzo

A humble island dwelling given a new life

Pantelleria, Sicily
Rosa Maria Borgia

In a country bursting with extravagant architecture and palatial homes, there are also hidden gems – humble yet charming spaces. Tenuta Borgia is one of the largest country estates on the island of Pantelleria; set within the Pantelleria National Park, the sprawling property covers 25 acres (10.1 hectares) on the southwest coast of the island. Scattered across the rolling hills are ancient *dammusi* – vernacular structures with thick, lava-stone walls and domed roofs that were built sometime around the 1700s as homes for local farmers.

The *dammusi* at Tenuta Borgia were brought back to life by Rosa Maria Borgia, a retired doctor, who restored the drystone structures with help from local architect Gabriella Giuntoli. The largest among the many buildings that occupy the estate is Dammuso Grande, a complex of two separate buildings connected by thoughtfully planned outdoor spaces peppered with citrus trees and

rose bushes. Borgia kept the interior of the house true to its simple roots – whitewashing the walls and using local materials. Clashing swathes of majolica tiles – traditional decorative ceramics from the south of Italy – line the floors and counter-tops, adding a sense of dynamism to the otherwise monastic space.

The furniture is a mix of antiques (a marble-topped kitchen table, a heavy wooden carved armoire and spindly cast-iron beds) and more modern pieces, like a set of simple white-and-blue De Padova sofas. In the living room, Borgia injected a touch of playfulness by hanging squid-shaped blown-glass sculptures made in Murano by the artist Maria Grazia Rosin. The *dammusi* now operate as guest houses, allowing visitors to discover the island's wild charms. The property was even immortalized in Luca Guadagnino's 2015 film *A Bigger Splash*.

1 The living room features a blown glass squid sculpture by the artist Maria Grazia Rosin.
2 Majolica tiles in the kitchen. 3 The grounds surrounding the house are planted with
olive trees. 4 Vaulted ceilings and arched doorways are typical features of traditional
Pantellerian *dammusi* dwellings.

A humble island dwelling given a new life

A richly-decorated brutalist villa

Florence
Dimorestudio

Florence may be best known for its extravagant Renaissance architecture, but the city also played an important role in the story of modern Italian design. The Tuscan capital was the birthplace of Radical Design, an avant-garde movement concerned with rebuking the bland tyranny of modernism. All of which is to say that forward-thinking architects and designers have long found a welcoming home in Florence, the Milan-based design firm Dimorestudio, led by Emiliano Salci and Britt Moran, among them.

Within the realm of contemporary Italian design, Dimorestudio is known for its extravagant interiors, rich in narrative and weighty historical references. Adept at seamlessly blending tradition with innovation, Salci and Moran brought their signature spirit of decadent anachronism to this brutalist villa, originally designed in 1964 by Florentine architect Franco Bonaiuti.

The villa tumbles over the crest of a hill overlooking the historic city; within, the designers responded by deftly playing with elevation and proportion, reflecting the hilly expanse outside the floor-to-ceiling windows. The living room, for instance, sits sunken below the main level and is accessed by three floating stone steps, a reference to architect Carlo Scarpa's 1958 Olivetti showroom in Venice's Piazza San Marco, which features a similar staircase at its centre.

Each room exists as its own indulgent vignette, as richly layered and carefully considered as a stage set. Next to the Scarpa-inspired steps hang two nineteenth-century painted panels from China, which overlook a Bruno Mathsson daybed from 1961 and a handwoven Mauritanian rug. In the dressing room, they conjured a *mise-en-scène* inspired by imagined opium dens, complete with a scarlet Willy Rizzo pouffe from the 1970s, silk Tai Ping carpet and botanical wallpaper, which lines the wardrobe doors. It is a mélange of styles and eras that feels intimately outside of time.

1 Rich jewel tones and antique-inspired materials add layers of intrigue. 2 A floral fabric-lined armoire and fuchsia Willy Rizzo pouffe from the 1970s give the dressing room a boudoir feel. 3 The living room features 19th-century Chinese panels, a 1961 Bruno Mathsson daybed and a burl wood table by Willy Rizzo.

An eclectic multigenerational creative abode

Milan
Piero Fornasetti
& Barnaba Fornasetti

Designer and illustrator Piero Fornasetti grew up in the house now known as Casa Fornasetti, located in the Città Studi district of Milan. It was here, in the ground-floor workshop, that he founded his eponymous company in 1940. What started as a simple idea – to screen- and lithograph-print his fantastical drawings onto furniture and ceramics – has blossomed into one of the most recognisable and storied Italian design brands still in operation today. Since Piero's passing in 1988, both the company and the family home have been under the creative direction of his only son, Barnaba, who has put his own imaginative spin on both.

Casa Fornasetti, where Barnaba still resides, is a living archive of the brand's past six decades. Indeed, the instantly recognisable illustrations animate almost every surface of the house. In the guest bedroom, where each object is rendered a dramatic shade of burgundy (thus decorated – according to Barnaba – so that visitors wouldn't

feel compelled to stay longer than three days), a velvet pillow depicts politely-dressed opera-goers at Milan's Teatro alla Scala theatre. A CD tower in the studio resembles a New York high-rise. A duo of collages in the office combine floating hot-air balloons with colourful kitchen utensils.

These familiar characters from Fornasetti's visual repertoire mingle with bizarre antiques and vintage bric-a-brac, creating a profoundly layered dwelling that would require extensive excavation to fully comprehend. But more than simply an unusual and eclectic abode, Casa Fornasetti represents the endless creativity of Italian design and its potential to endure across generations.

1 An assemblage of Fornasetti objects and collected ephemera in the study and library.
2 Piero Fornasetti founded his eponymous brand here, in the home's ground-floor
workshop. 3 The guest bedroom is painted entirely in a garish shade of red, supposedly
to discourage guests from staying for too long. 4 The music room is filled with
Fornasetti-branded CD towers, furnishings and musical instruments.

An eclectic multigenerational creative abode

A countryside estate with a nod to its past

San Corrado di Fuori, Sicily
Corrado Papa

For centuries the Kingdom of Sicily was ruled over by a mosaic of influential families who presided over a complex agricultural feudal system. Wealthy clans accumulated riches, while the peasants residing in their fiefdoms worked the land. The system ended in the nineteenth century, but vestiges remain in the form of opulent villas, many of which belonged to these dynasties. The Di Lorenzos – otherwise known as the Marquises of Castelluccio – were one of the oldest and most influential of these families; they ruled over the fiefdom of San Lorenzo, between the towns of Noto and Pachino, from their main residence in the town of Castelluccio. During the summertime the family retreated to what is now known as Villa Ruiz, a nineteenth-century neoclassical palazzo in the rural hamlet of San Corrado di Fuori.

In 2011 the villa was purchased by a foreign-born film producer, who sought to restore the summer retreat to its former glory. They entrusted local architect Corrado Papa with the restoration. In an effort to keep the historic villa as true to its original design as possible, very little of the nineteenth-century layout was changed. Instead, Papa and his team highlighted the home's original features. The soft limestone floors and patterned ceramic tiles were cleaned and polished. The trompe l'oeil frescos were touched up. What was once the ground-floor kitchen was transformed into an expansive bath-room, with the original stone cistern left *in situ*.

In furnishing the house, the owner sourced objects and antiques that spoke to Sicily's fascinating decorative traditions. Centuries-old sculptures and Baroque-style furniture mingle in the grand entranceway, while paintings depicting Southern Italy's infamous volcanoes – Stromboli, Etna and Vesuvius – line the walls.

1 The villa was once the summer house of the Marquises of Castelluccio. 2 Sicilian baroque antiques in the entranceway. 3 Trompe l'oeil festooned curtains on the walls of one of the sitting rooms. 4 A carved wooden four-poster bed and patterned wallpaper in the guest room.

A countryside estate with a nod to its past

A punkish take on Italian style

Milan
Concorde

Milan has always been known as a cold city. Its northern location and endless grey facades have left it with a mystique of bourgeois impenetrability. Unlike chaotic Rome or historic Florence, the city's character can be described as restrained, orderly, impeccably turned out – all descriptors that can also be applied to its homes. The Milan-based design studio Concorde, led by Carlo Prada and Nelly Hoffmann, sought to turn that conservative reputation on its head with the design of Prada's apartment on the first floor of a classically Milanese building from the 1930s.

Leaving the architecture – the original parquet wooden floors and intricately moulded ceilings – largely intact, Prada and Hoffmann aimed to corrupt the bourgeois atmosphere by working with urban materials and bringing outdoor elements inside. Rubber flooring (the same used in Milan's subway system), synthetic grass, PVC panels, building-site netting and punk studs were used in

place of conventional domestic furnishings like curtains or carpets. Another crucial element of the home is Prada's collection of design pieces from the 1980s to the 2000s: a transparent dining table by Enzo Mari; a corrugated glass cabinet by Ron Arad; and a floor lamp by the architect Renzo Piano.

Set against these modern and industrial components are relics from the past. Religious figurines are scattered around the home or placed in niches carved into the walls, while heavy, wrought-iron antiques juxtapose with the classic architecture. On the walls hang Baroque portraits and Dutch still life paintings, upending the techno aesthetic with a sense of medieval drama.

1 An AEO lounge chair by the 1960s radical design group Archizoom and a set of netted side tables by Concorde in the living room. 2 A flower-shaped table by Cattelan Italia and sofa by Rodolfo Dordoni for Driade. 3 The bedroom features faux grass carpeting, a glass bedside table by Ron Arad for Fiam and a bed by Adolfo Natalini for Driade. 4 A Juliette chair by Hannes Wettstein and custom steel cabinets in the kitchen.

A punkish take on Italian style

An art-filled former convent

Florence
Tommaso Bencistà Falorni
& Matteo Andretta

The Italian city exists in layers; from the Roman era onwards, urban landscapes have often evolved by strata, especially in an ancient city like Florence. The apartment of Matteo Andretta, a fashion designer, and Tommaso Bencistà Falorni, the owner of a PR and event agency, reflects this complex heritage. Located on Via Ghibellina, the longest street in the historic centre, the building was originally part of a sixteenth-century convent. Later, in the 1950s, it was transformed into an artisan's workshop, but remnants of its past lives remain.

In designing the space, the couple's goal was to create an eye-catching environment that was functional in daily life yet suited to hosting large groups of friends. That challenge was more than met in the sumptuous living room. The space is crowned by the convent's original ribbed vaults and intricately decorated capitals. Beneath the arched ceiling, the couple designed a custom, horseshoe-shaped velvet sofa inspired by the 1970s; it hugs the room's

perimeter and can accommodate at least twelve people. A collection of objects and art – picked up from local antique markets or given as gifts by creative friends – is displayed around the white-walled room.

The apartment's walls are mostly neutral, save for in the bedroom, which features a custom-made trompe l'oeil-effect wallpaper with imagery sourced from a bedroom in a Veneto castle, the walls of which had been painted with a landscape mural. The home's most striking feature, however, is its terrace, lushly adorned with leafy plants and flowers. Surrounded entirely by windows, the terrace blends the indoors and outdoors, creating a serene connection between the interior living space and the natural beauty of the surrounding environment.

1 A painting by Silvio Loffredo hangs in the guest room. 2 In the neutral-toned living room a 2021 painting by Samuele Alfani provides a shock of colour. 3 The apartment wraps around a leafy central terrace. 4 A self-portrait by Cesar Santos and an Artemide Tolomeo lamp sit on the bed's wooden headboard.

An art-filled former convent

A waterfront home that celebrates its original features

Venice
Fabrizio Casiraghi

The Dorsoduro neighbourhood of Venice, a tangle of narrow canals and even narrower streets near the western bank of the Grand Canal, has long been a haven for artists and artisans. Away from the crowds of Piazza San Marco, one can still glimpse the workings of everyday Venetian life in the quiet restaurants, curious bookshops and local galleries. It's here that, for several generations, the Parisian entrepreneur Julien Desselle's family has kept a small apartment overlooking the Ca' Rezzonico museum. In 2018 Deselle asked the architect Fabrizio Casiraghi to revive the canal-side home. According to the architect, his intention for the space was to integrate Desselle's wide array of personal collections into an inviting space that will endure stylistically.

Casiraghi made a concerted effort to preserve the home's fine original details, like the original *terrazzo* flooring, which shifts from white to red to blue as one traverses the apartment. He elevated these elements with sleek modern furnishings, like a petrol-blue kitchen with brass detailing, anchored by an ink-toned marble counter.

Desselle's objects range from the ancient – Baroque-style consoles in the hallway, an Asian embroidered silk tapestry in the bedroom – to the modern. A rare set of Gaetano Pesce artworks is displayed on the entrance staircase, while the bedroom features engraved metal artworks by Piero Fornasetti. In the living room, a sculpture of Julien's father is showcased next to a velvet Azucena sofa and armchair, Barovier & Toso crystal sconces, a painting by Sam Francis and an old wooden desk owned by the family.

1 Brass detailing borders the green marble worktop in the kitchen. 2 An eighteenth-century Chinese screen hangs behind a white vintage Azucena Pinacoteca sofa.
3 An antique portrait in the modern bathroom. 4 A baroque chair in the corner of the bedroom.

A waterfront home that celebrates its original features

A vibrant apartment with old-world charm

Milan
Tamu McPherson

In Italy, everything is a family affair; from obligatory Sunday lunches to dynastic businesses, kin rules almost every aspect of life. It's a well-known fact, for example, that the country's best apartments rarely go on the market. Instead, they are passed down from generation to fortunate generation. That was the case for Jamaica-born editor and lifestyle influencer Tamu McPherson, who inherited an apartment full of old-world charm from her stylish Italian mother-in-law. The sprawling flat boasts all the trappings of pedigreed Milanese domestic architecture. Beneath a vaulted ceiling, finely hewn *boiserie* lines the walls of the office. Stately moulding adds a sense of proportion to the octagonal living room. The dining room's mosaic flooring depicts a family crest, suggesting a noble history.

Some of the apartment's exceptional furniture was also gifted to McPherson by her mother-in-law – the Luigi Caccia Dominioni sofas in the living room and steel dining table by Carlo Scarpa, for instance –

but the aesthetic is genuinely her own. A lover of all things colourful, she first laid a muted canvas of pear green, sky blue and dusty pink paint on the walls. That allowed the furniture – one-off pieces from local galleries and reupholstered vintage seating in vivid shades of fuchsia and aquamarine – to pop. The next layer was her searingly cool collection of contemporary art, including paintings by Francesco Vaccarone and Marcel Cordeiro.

A vibrant apartment with old-world charm

A vibrant apartment with old-world charm

1 Macpherson's mother-in-law gifted her the vintage steel dining table by Carlo Scarpa.
2 In the living room, sofas by Knoll and Luigi Caccia Dominioni. 3 The kitchen has
a more muted colour palette. 4 The home's entranceway. 5 Pop-coloured vintage
furniture stands out against the stately wood *boiserie* in the office.

Index

Page references in *italics* indicate illustrations

Photography credits

Adam Štěch: 172-177, 206-209

Andrea Ferrari: 236-239

Andrea Wyner: 216-219, 232-235

Carola Ripamonti: 210-215

Danilo Scarpati: 46-51, 78-83, 130-135

Denise Bonetti: 166-171

DePasquale+Maffini: 102-107

DePasquale+Maffini; styling by Francesca Santambrogio: 94-97

DePasquale+Maffini; styling by Martina Lucatelli: 124-129

Federico Floriani: 248-251

Francesco Dolfo: 84-89, 188-193, 220-223, 228-231

Francesco Dolfo; production by Benedetta Rossi Albini: 194-199, 252-255

Francesco Dolfo; styling by Sophie Wannenes: 146-149

François Halard: 108-111

Giulio Ghirardi: 4, 6, 12-17, 112-117, 150-155

James Mollison: 200-205

Luca De Santis: 142-145

Marina Denisova: 224-227

Marsý Hild Þórsdóttir: back cover image, 66-71

Mattia Aquila: 244-247

Mirko Morelli: 62-65

Nathalie Krag: 24-27

Paola Pansini: 52-57

Romain Laprade: 256-259

Salva López: front cover image, 28-33, 034-39, 160-165, 266, 270

Sarah Magni: 9, 18-23, 178-181

Serena Eller Vainicher: 182-187

Sofie Delauw: 58-61

Stefan Giftthaler: 10-11, 40-45, 72-77, 90-93, 118-123, 136-141, 156-159 (© DACS 2024), 240-243

Valentina Sommariva: 98-101, 260-265

1 The view from the roof of the home designed by Andrew Trotter and Marcelo Martínez in Soleto, Puglia (*see page 160*).
2 A glimpse of Venice's Grand Canal as seen from the side of the palazzo owned by Vincenzo De Cotiis (*see page 28*).

Phaidon Press Limited
2 Cooperage Yard
London E15 2QR

Phaidon Press Inc.
111 Broadway
New York, NY 10006

phaidon.com

First published 2024
© 2024 Phaidon Press Limited

ISBN 978 1 83866 866 2

A CIP catalogue record for this book is available
from the British Library and the Library of Congress.

Commissioning Editor: Emilia Terragni
Executive Editor: Joe Pickard
Production Controller: Zuzana Cimalova
Graphic Design: Apartamento Studios
& Mariana Martín Zumárraga

Printed in China

Cover images
Front: The Venice home of Vincenzo De Cotiis
shot by Salva López, featuring the artwork
Satin Ions (Weak), 2017 by Nina Canell
©Nina Canell/DACS London, IVARO Dublin, 2024
Back: Roberto Baciocchis home in Arezzo
shot by Marsý Hild Þórsdóttir